# Bags

## *Helping Your Kids Lighten the Load*

CHRIS SASSER

**D6 FAMILY MINISTRY**
114 BUSH RD · NASHVILLE, TN 37217 · 800.877.7030 · D6FAMILY.COM

*BAGS: Helping Your Kids Lighten the Load*

© 2022 by Chris Sasser

Published by Randall House & D6 Family Ministries
114 Bush Road
Nashville, TN 37217

Visit www.randallhouse.com

All Scripture quotations are taken from the HOLY BIBLE, NEW INTERNATIONAL VERSION® NIV® Copyright © 1973, 1978, 1984, 2011 by Biblica, Inc.®. Used by permission. All rights reserved worldwide. (http://www.biblica.com/biblica-about-us/terms-of-use/)

13-ISBN 9781614841203

Printed in the United States of America

# Table of Contents

# Introduction

*"Let us throw off everything that hinders and the sin that so easily entangles. And let us run with perseverance the race marked out for us" (Hebrews 12:1b).*

Not to tell you something you don't already know, but this parenting thing is hard. As I've said many times (and heard other people say), these little bundles of joy that God gives us do not come with instruction manuals, and they do not stay little for long. Once they become a part of our family, everything changes. We spend the next 20-30 years (maybe longer) just trying to navigate everything from sippy cups to car insurance. It's exhausting. But it's also amazing! God has entrusted us with the life and well-being of another human, or two, or three, or more (we're praying for you folks!). We get to be on a journey of life and faith that will truly have an impact on generations to come.

As we step into this conversation together, there are a few things you need to know about me:

I am: A child. Obviously, I have parents and I have been on the other side of the parenting equation for all my life. My dad passed away a few years ago, but my mom is still going strong and she is incredible. I'm over 50, and she still likes to parent. I am sure some of you can relate.

1

I am: A husband and a parent. I have been married to my wife Karin since 2002, and we have two amazing kids, CJ and Kylie. We've been through the infant, toddler, and elementary school phases, and we are now knee-deep in the teenage years. I am trying to figure it all out for myself and my family.

I am: A pastor. I have been in full-time ministry for almost 30 years in youth and children's ministry, and I have been serving as a family ministry pastor for almost 15 years with a growing focus on helping parents. I want everyone in my family to love and follow Jesus, and I want everyone in your family to love and follow Jesus too. I desperately want redemption for kids, parents, and families.

Most of my passion for this project flows from the last two, parent and pastor.

I am *not*: An expert. A ministry friend of mine once told me that anyone who claims to be a parenting expert is probably not a parent. Instead of listening to them, you should turn and run.

I am *not*: A finished product. I don't have it all figured out. This parenting thing is a process, and I'm learning, changing, missing the mark, and growing every day.

I am *not*: Giving up! I will not back down from this quest to be a better parent and help others do the same. It's just too important!

## *What Does Successful Parenting Look Like?*

If you were to sit down with a group of parents and ask them, "What does success look like in parenting?" you would get different answers. Most people want their kids to experience worldly success and live the "American dream" whatever that is. We can all so easily become focused on that. We fall into the trap of believing our job is to help our kids get good grades, get into the right college, get a good job, become good citizens, marry the right person, have the right friends, make good money, and the list goes on. We want them to be "successful" in the world's eyes. All of that is good stuff (at least most of it) and all things I want for my kids. But what is the goal in Christian parenting? What are we aiming for in raising our kids?

As I've worked my way through this project, I've come up with a bit of a different target. You see, I know a lot of adults who have achieved worldly success, who have chased the American dream, and who are still so very empty. They have worked hard for years and years to provide for themselves and their family, but they have missed so much along the way. They have chased after things of this world and have sought to build their own kingdom with a false sense of stability. As I think about my kids and what I want for them and their future, I've landed on a few things.

## *I want my kids to be healthy.*

The obvious first thought is for them to be physically healthy, but I only have a certain amount of control over that one. Aside from that, what I really want is for them to be mentally, emotionally, relationally, and spiritually healthy. I want them to have a strong mind where they have the confidence to think on their own. I want them to be able to stand up in the face of difficulty and not be thrown by the wind and the waves of life. I want my children to be able to look people in the eye and have a real, face-to-face conversation that can lead them to deeper relationships. I want them to have a real understanding that there is a God in Heaven Who is the author and perfecter of all things. I want them to know this same God is pursuing them, and they can pursue Him back.

3

I once had a wise mentor tell me that one of the goals in parenting is to have a *real* relationship with your kids when they are in their 20s. That's what I want! After having talked to countless young adults who don't have a real relationship with their parents and feeling their pain, I agree with my friend. It's the idea of "keeping the end in mind" as we travel along our family journey. I can't influence someone with whom I don't have a relationship, and my kids will need my influence in their young adult (and older adult) years.

## *I want my kids to know and love Jesus!*

We've been praying this for them since they were born. So much of what we try to do in our parenting points to this. We don't have a lot of Bible studies and family devotions in our house, but we really do try to have a Deuteronomy 6 mentality with our kids.

> Hear, O Israel: The Lord our God, the Lord is one. Love the Lord your God with all your heart and with all your soul and with all your strength. These commandments that I give you today are to be on your hearts. Impress them on your children. Talk about them when you sit at home and when you walk along the road, when you lie down and when you get up. Tie them as symbols on your hands and bind them on your foreheads. Write them on the doorframes of your houses and on your gates (Deuteronomy 6:4-9).

So again, you *have* to determine, what is the goal in raising your kids?

*The premise of this book is that our kids are packing and carrying with them some enormous emotional baggage they have no idea how to deal with.* This baggage weighs them down and often keeps them from living lives that are mentally, emotionally, relationally, and spiritually healthy. As they move into their young adult years, their baggage frequently keeps them from being able to live life under the grace and freedom God provides. As they try to take steps forward in their faith, their bags weigh them down and hold them back in so many ways. These bags come from all areas of life and can be packed by a wide range of people.

Friends pack bags. Teachers pack bags. Coaches pack bags. Pastors and youth leaders pack bags. And yes, parents pack bags too. I am learning, in both my own experience and in what I know about others, that we as parents are often not aware of the bags our kids are packing. We may know that something is going on and they are struggling, but we have no idea the depth of pain our kids' emotional bags cause and the long-lasting effects they can have. In some ways, this is a book about awareness and preventative maintenance.

Although I believe we must fight against our kids packing these emotional bags, I know their bags are not the total sum of who they will become. Getting this stuff right does not necessarily equal perfect kids—nothing does. There is so much more to growing up, and this book could never come close to covering it all. This concept is yet another tool we can use as parents to help our kids grow along the way.

Finally, I want you to know this book is rooted in my faith in God through Jesus. In every chapter, you will read about biblical principles that play into our emotional health. I believe teaching our kids to follow Jesus is critical and plays a huge role in their overall development. You'll also read about practical, simple ideas we as parents often forget. As I have been working on this project over the past several years, it has literally changed the way I parent. I see things I didn't see before because I am looking at my kids and their development through a new lens. I truly hope you can see what is happening with your kids, and I pray this book will lead you to help them lighten the load.

As you work through each chapter and reflect on the questions provided, I suggest you record your thoughts and answers in a journal. (Get more resources and download a free guide at www.thebagsbook. com.) How we answer these questions and the changes we make in our parenting can have a lasting impact on our kids. I hope you will revisit these concepts every few years as your kids move into different phases of their lives. Thinking through and recording our thoughts are worth the time and effort!

Take a few minutes to think about what "success" looks like for you as a parent. Write down some specific things you want to aim for as you raise your kids. What are the top five values and principles you want your kids to have embraced by the time they move out of your home?

## Chapter One
# Just Don't Pack!

*"We really need our parents to take the time to learn and understand the source of our baggage."—young adult*

As we wrapped up dinner and headed to the living room, the mood was light. We had just spent an hour or so laughing, joking, and enjoying the company of this young couple. We had talked about jobs and sports and life and friends. Although my wife and I often looked forward to these sessions, I knew that after dinner the mood would change, and things might get a little uncomfortable. We were about to dive into a deep conversation about real life and serious issues. We needed to get to the bottom of some things.

On this particular night, the young man was someone whom I had known for quite a while. His family had been involved in our church for years in many different ways. He had a number of siblings, and I knew them all incredibly well. As their youth pastor, I had walked with them through years of family drama. As our session that evening moved along, he proceeded to back up the dump truck and unload it on us. Mom and dad had recently divorced, and most of the kids were struggling in different ways. I knew about the years of tension and strife, but I honestly had no idea of the depth of pain and anger this young man carried. For over a decade they had seemed like a typical,

7

healthy, American, Christian family. But under the surface, so much more was going on. He proceeded to share about his constant power struggle with his dad, his disappointment and anger with his mom, and his overall disconnect with his siblings. As this young man was embarking on the next phase of his life with his future spouse, he was carrying a bag of burdens that was weighing heavily on his soul.

Over the past fifteen years or so, my wife and I have spent many nights like this one with young couples who are on their way to marriage. We have a pre-marital counseling process where we take them through a series of conversations to help them uncover the major issues they may face in their lives together. We start with just getting to know them better and hearing their stories. It's amazing what they will share with us in just the first session. We really start to dig deep in session two. We ask them questions about their childhood and their teen years. We hear stories about their families and their parents. We learn about their hobbies and interests, their dreams and aspirations. Always, and I mean always, we hear about their bags.

You know about bags. Bags are those big bulky things that we all carry with us as we travel…through life. I'm not talking about bags full of candy or a bag full of clothes packed for an exciting family vacation. I'm talking about emotional bags that are often big, heavy, and hard to unpack. These bags that start to fill up early in life can have profound impacts on the way we see the world and how we live. The bags are painful and often stay in storage for years and years. For some, they last for a lifetime.

We all pack bags throughout our lives. It seems to be inevitable. We'll go through situations and circumstances that create memories and shape who we are. People will say things to us, do things to us, and treat us in a certain way. Oftentimes bags get packed through an ongoing deposit of one item after another with a decreasing resistance to the packing process.

A coach tells a player that he or she is not good enough to start on the team, and this gets reinforced day after day as the kid goes to practice after practice but doesn't get to play—bag packed.

A teacher criticizes a student because he or she isn't good in that particular subject and might not "have what it takes" to get into college—bag packed.

A friend plans a sleepover with most of the girls on the soccer team, but one girl gets left out and watches the party unfold on social media—bag packed.

A parent creates situations at home where one sibling is subtly compared to another in behavior, school, or sports—bag packed.

A teen gets caught up in the moment with a boyfriend or girlfriend and makes some sexual choices he or she soon regrets—bag packed.

You know these bags. You packed some of them as you moved along your journey of life and, if you look closely, your kids are packing them now. As we hear from these young adults in our counseling sessions, I've often wondered what their parents would say. My wife and I have joked about what our kids will be saying to someone else when they are in some sort of counseling when they are in their 20s. But at some point in my journey as a parent, it dawned on me: Do my kids have to pack these bags?

That question is what has driven me to step into this project. As I have done research and talked to kids, teens, and young adults about the struggles of life, I am more convinced than ever that our kids need help. Many prominent voices have begun to sound the alarm about a "mental health crisis" that has emerged in our society, and our kids and teens are right in the middle of it. I wonder if, for years, we as parents and leaders simply tried to push our kids through the difficulties of life, not taking the time to truly understand what was happening to them. I have come to believe that we don't need to push them through it, we need to help them through it. We need to help them, as much as we can, steer away from accumulating baggage that will weigh them down and inhibit their ability to step into their true identity in Christ and live the life God has for them. So, let's dive a little deeper into my question: Do my kids have to pack these bags?

While I can take ownership of a lot of things when it comes to the way I parent my kids, I know I can't completely control what happens to them in life. I can't control what they see, what they hear, or how they are treated by others in the world. I can't always control what bags get packed and how big these bags are. I can, however, decide to actively work against my kids packing these bags that could weigh them down for a lifetime. What if there are things I can do as a parent that will help stop these crippling bags before they get packed and possibly help my kids pack something else? We all know that it's often much harder to undo something than it is to never let it take root at all, especially when it comes to emotional issues.

As I searched for information on this topic, I found articles and books on how to deal with the emotional baggage of our past. When it comes to emotional baggage, I found techniques for unloading, dealing with, getting rid of, unpacking, and dumping your bags. All these ideas presuppose something about these emotional bags: that they have to be packed in the first place. As I started digging into this project, I saw a picture and quote that said, "Emotional Baggage— Don't worry, everyone has it."

Okay, so we are all going to accumulate some sort of baggage as we grow up. I get that. As a die-hard optimist (who was once called "stupidly optimistic" by a good friend), I have to ask: does this have to be the case for our kids? Does this have to be the reality for our families? I understand we can't totally prevent some bags from being packed, but does that mean we shouldn't try? Instead of giving in to the idea we are all going to pack some heavy bags that will weigh us down, can we possibly do some things to steer our kids away from the negative baggage that is so prevalent and help them become emotionally and spiritually healthier as they grow up? Have we as a culture decided this is a war we cannot win, so we just do not want to fight? If we decide we do want to fight, do we know where to start and how to fight effectively?

I want to set up my kids for success in the future! I want them to embrace their identities in Christ, and I want to have solid relationships with them when they are adults. Over my years of life and ministry, I have learned one thing about our emotional baggage: as people grow older, the impact of our baggage gets greater and greater. I have seen this over and over again: Kids and teens who pack bags become adults who don't know how to deal with the pain of these bags. Because of this, they struggle relationally, emotionally, and spiritually. Frequently bags get packed so full they eventually burst—and that's never pretty.

Let me explain it this way. Our pastor, Mike Ashcraft, came up with a great concept we have used at our church that can help us understand the importance of this idea.

*En*　　　　　　*F*　　　　　　*Ex*

En = Encounter　F = Formation　Ex = Expression

We all *encounter* things in our lives through our everyday experiences.

Our encounters play a huge role in *forming* who we are and will be in the future.

11

How we are formed will play out in how we live our lives, in our *expression*.

From the time we are born, we begin to set patterns in what we think, what we say, what we do, how we operate, and ultimately, who we are. This is also true for our kids. So, if what our kids encounter forms who they are and how they react, wouldn't it stand to reason that we might want to pay more attention to what is happening to them?

Dream with me for a minute. What if, as a parent, I knew the most common bags that get packed over the years a child grows up, let's say from age 5 to 25? What if I not only knew the most common negative bags kids pack during these years, but what if I could *actively* work against my kids packing those bags?

What if I could be *intentional* in my parenting to help my kids *not* pack these bags? What if I could help them navigate circumstances in their lives in such a way that it minimizes the amount of negative baggage they pack? What difference would that make in my kids' lives when they become young adults? Would it change how they think? Would it change how they trust? Would it shape what they believe, who they marry, and how they one day operate as parents? Would it change the type of people they become?

If they could go into their young adult years (and then into their adult lives) *without* a ton of heavy baggage, would they be healthier emotionally, relationally, and spiritually? Would the success I am looking for as a parent be more likely? Would my kids be better off?

I think they would, and that's what I want for my kids! Sure, I want them to have good grades, go to a good college, get a good job, find the right spouse, and have all of the success in the world. But I *really* want them to be healthy deep down inside! I want them to have peace and stability. I don't want them to have to deal with all the pain and stress it takes to carry around deep, emotional baggage, partially because I think oftentimes the enemy uses that baggage to pull us away from the abundant life we can have in Jesus. Ultimately, I want my kids to know and love God, to understand their identities in Christ, and to live from that place of freedom, not being weighed down by unnecessary baggage.

Can God's grace and mercy overcome the bags we carry and redeem them in our lives? Absolutely! Does God have a purpose for struggles, trials, and even suffering in our lives? Absolutely! But what if our kids didn't have to go through years of unnecessary pain, struggle, and confusion because of the emotional baggage they pack as they travel through childhood and adolescence? What if we, as their parents, could learn to help our kids navigate the struggles they are bound to face in a healthy way that could prevent them from packing bags that have long-term consequences? What if we could help them turn their negative encounters into tools that can be used to form them positively and lead them to the lives they long to live?

Over the last few years, as I've been looking at life through this lens, I've talked to a lot of people about their bags. I've reflected on almost 30 years of working with kids, teens, and families. I've done focus groups with college students and young adults. I've talked to people in their twenties to people in their seventies. I've taken numerous notes and I've learned a ton. In one of my focus groups, a young adult made a great observation, "Not packing the bags has to start with knowing what they are." Bingo!

Through this process, I've identified eight common bags kids pack:

- The Relational Bag—With parents, siblings, and peers
- The Performance Bag—In school and sports and with friends
- The Identity Bag—Struggle to understand identity, belonging, and purpose
- The Comparison Bag—Starts with siblings and moves to peers and the world
- The Authority Bag—Wrestling with who is in charge of the decisions in my life
- The Rejection Bag—From peers, teams, groups, and family
- The Guilt and Shame Bag—About what I have done and what has been done to me
- The Disappointment Bag—Dealing with disappointment and learning through failure

Each of these bags can lead to varying levels of anxiety and depression.

*This book is an encouragement to parents to take the time and effort to be aware of what's happening to your kids and be their guardians in more than just the traditional sense.* Because of my role as a pastor, I'm around a lot of teenagers, college students, young adults, and parents. I see the effects of this baggage almost every day. I beg you to do whatever you can to help your kids guard their hearts and their minds as they grow and mature and help them steer clear of this emotional baggage that can have real, long-term effects.

*This is a call to parents to take the time and effort to point our kids in the right direction and lead them to full and abundant lives.* This will require you to be more aware of what you say and how you treat these precious gifts God has given you. You will have to pay close attention to what is going on in their lives outside the home, and you will have to work hard to redirect many of their thoughts and actions. It will take sacrifice, discernment, strength, and resolve as you seek to deposit in your children the life-giving values that will lead them down a path of true life.

*These ideas are rooted in my faith in God through Jesus.* In every chapter, you will read about biblical principles that play into our emotional health. Teaching your kids to follow Jesus is critical and plays a huge role in their overall development.

*This book is about awareness and preventive maintenance.* If you know about the bags your kids might be packing, you can try to do something about them. Although I believe you must fight against your kids packing these emotional bags, there is so much more to life that will play into who our kids become and so much more that we need to pay attention to as parents. But what if you could use what is written here to prevent much of what your kids could pack over the years? This "bags" concept is just another tool you can use as a parent to help your kids grow along the way.

As we transition into discussing the common bags, you'll notice that many of them overlap. Life is complicated with many layers, and our emotional state is no different. This list of bags is not exhaustive; it's just a compilation of what I have seen over the years and heard the most in my conversations. I've also learned that not every child will pack every bag, which is why it is so important to pay attention and be incredibly aware of what is going on in the lives of our children. Depending on how old your kids are, you may find yourself thinking, "It's too late! My kids have already packed that one." If you find yourself feeling that way, I encourage you to dig in and know that *it's never too late*. It's never too late to fight for health and to fight for your child to go in a different direction. The strategy will be different if your kids are older than if they are younger, but a bag that is only halfway packed is always easier to stop packing (or unpack) than one that is already full. You simply have to decide whether or not it's worth the fight, and you know it is.

Before we jump in, I want to say one more thing. You already intuitively know a lot of what you are about to read. You do. You've lived it yourself as you've grown up, and if you look closely, you'll be able to see your children living it right now no matter what their age. As parents, you need to be aware that the bags you packed growing up will affect how you deal with the bags your kids are packing. As you read more, you may discover you need to do some real work to sort through your own baggage. That's another whole book (or series of books). I would encourage you to pay attention to the emotions that surface as you reflect on the bags you have accumulated over the years. You may find that you need to talk to a counselor, pastor, or trusted friend. For our purposes, you simply need to know that your past very much plays into how your kids are experiencing you, and they may be packing some of the same bags you did.

Each chapter is broken into three parts. First, I'll identify the bag by telling stories and sharing observations from my life, research, and years of ministry. I'll then give a few simple bullet points of the potential pitfalls of each bag being packed. My list won't be complete, but it will get you thinking about what might be happening to your kids if these bags get packed. You will have to keep an eye on your kids to discern whether they are experiencing these effects. I'll finish each chapter by giving you a few practical suggestions on how to prevent your children from packing the specific bag and perhaps pack something else. The third section of each chapter might be the most valuable part you read. I hope and pray that we as parents can pay attention to what is happening to our kids as they grow up in today's world. I pray this book will help you lighten your children's loads so they may enter adulthood with less negative baggage and grow to be healthy adults.

## Reflection Questions

As you look back at your life, can you identify some "bags" you have packed along the way? List some of these bags and briefly detail how these bags have impacted you.

Do you think you are aware of what is really going on with your kids as they grow up? How can you stay current with them as they move through their life?

Do you feel like you have an intentional "preventative maintenance" plan to help your kids minimize their baggage and "lighten the load" as they grow up? What are some things you already do to help your kids with their "bags?"

## Chapter Two
# The Relational Bag

*"I don't even want to bother with love because I've never seen a successful relationship."—young adult*

When I heard this statement from a young adult in my church, my heart sank. I knew a little bit about his story, but I had no idea that the relational baggage he was carrying was so heavy. He's such a great guy, always smiling, always laughing, and seemingly all put together. He has a good job, good friends, a solid faith, and everything you would think a guy in his twenties would want. But if you dig a little deeper, you learn he is carrying the same burdens so many others carry.

One of the heaviest bags kids are packing today is what I call the "relational bag." This bag revolves around the sadness and disappointment kids have because of the state of the key relationships in their lives. In my focus groups, I heard student after student talk about the pain that comes with navigating relationships. Kids, youth, and young adults have unmet expectations and unsettling tension they do not know how to deal with. They have a real fear about their future potential for connection, friendship, and intimacy. Scripture consistently points to the idea we are created to support one another and live in community. Hebrews 10:24-25 says, "And let us consider how we may spur one another on toward love and good deeds, not giving up meeting together, as some are in the habit of doing, but encouraging one another—and all the more as you see the Day approaching." (Consider also Romans 12:16; 1 Corinthians 12:25-27; Philippians 2:4; 1 Thessalonians 5:14.)

Our experience with how to build and navigate relationships starts in the home and then extends to others around us. Because of the complexity of our relationships, this is one of a few bags that has several layers. When it comes to the *relational bag*, kids are packing this bag with their parents, their siblings, and their friends.

## *Relationships With Parents*

It started sometime early in his high school career. Mark had become a part of the youth group as a freshman or sophomore through some of his friends. He was the kind of kid who always had a smile on his face and was a true joy to be around. He was a great athlete and incredibly smart. He was a handsome guy, and he had a great girlfriend. He was popular, funny, and everyone knew he had an amazing future ahead. As Mark and I got closer through youth group, Bible studies, mission trips, and other activities, at some point he stopped calling me "Sass" (my nickname) and started calling me something else—"Dad"—which was weird, because I knew his dad! They seemed to have a great family and I thought Mark had a good relationship with his parents. Over the next few years, things would get tough, his parents would get a divorce, and I would learn a lot more about what was really going on in Mark's heart and mind.

When I ask young adults to talk about their families, they almost always start with their relationships with their parents. Sometimes these relationships are good with deep roots and strong ties. When it comes to thinking and talking about our relationships with our parents, we often harbor some sort of pain and disappointment. I frequently heard something like, "I love my parents, but..." Young adults acknowledge there is a certain functionality to their relationship with their parents, but there frequently seems to be an underlying sadness that these relationships weren't, and aren't, all they could be. I recognize one of the hard things about being a parent is that, as our kids grow up, we are all going to disappoint them. It's just part of the deal. It is a part of our fallen nature. However, I do know our kids deeply desire to have a real connection with us as their parents, and I wonder: Do they have to come out of the other side of their adolescent journeys with so much pain associated with their relationships with their parents? Do they have to have parental relational baggage?

One of the things that surprised me as I talked to so many kids and young adults is the fact that a lot of them are wondering, "Do my parents care about me because they have to (because it's part of the job description of being a parent), or do they care about me because they care about me?"

You might want to read that again. Our kids are growing up trying to figure out if we as parents love them. They know we are trying to guide them, direct them, teach them, and keep them out of trouble. They feel that in the ways we correct, discipline, push, and prod. They sometimes wonder if our incessant need to help them improve is more about us and our reputations than it is about them and their well-being. One young adult female shared, "My conversations with my mom always revolve around what I can do better. It's non-stop correction."

Did you catch that? She's a young adult who is in her twenties. She has a good job. She is "successful" in many ways. She is deeply involved in church. And her mom is non-stop correcting her—still!

As parents, we need to know that, in some ways, our kids are evaluating their potential to have a healthy marriage, healthy families, and healthy relationships based on what they see from and experience with us. One young adult said, "Your relationship with your parents plays into every relationship you will ever have." Kids today are struggling with love, and they are trying to understand what it is and how it behaves. They're not quite sure if they are getting real love from their parents, and this haunts them.

One college student said, "My parents had zero awareness about me. They taught the 'morals,' but since we didn't have a relationship, we never had real conversations." The first bag that kids pack is a Relational Bag with their parents.

## *Relationships With Siblings*

There really is such a thing as sibling rivalry (in case you didn't know). Shane was a senior in high school, a great soccer player, and absolutely brilliant. I had gotten to know him a little bit through his involvement in our church, and I was very impressed. I knew Shane had siblings, but I didn't know anything about them or anything about his parents. As the focus group he was in shifted to conversations about family, Shane told a story that spoke volumes. He shared that often, in public, his parents would talk about his brother's achievements. His brother must have been very successful, and his parents wanted to brag about their son. In his normal, soft-spoken voice, Shane shared that when his parents would talk about all that his brother was doing, it did something in him. It made him not like his brother.

If you have been blessed with more than one child, you know that sibling rivalries are real. They don't always rise to the level of fist fights, blood, or mean-girl gossip, but they are a normal part of family life. As parents, we have to be aware of the fact that our kids are packing relational bags with each other, and it starts at an early age. Toddlers fight over toys and, as parents, we have to referee. If I tell my son to give the toy to my daughter, he is not only upset with me, but he is furious with his sister. When that same son becomes a teenager and calls "shotgun" so he can sit in the front seat of the car, his sister is not happy with anyone because she has to sit in the back. These countless interactions between siblings that occur day after day, year after year can pack some serious bags that will have a deep impact on their relationships in the future. As parents, we have to be aware of how we subtly play into our kids packing this bag and how we can work to minimize its impact.

Because of proximity, immaturity, the desire for attention, and the need to be loved, kids are packing a sibling relational bag, and we have to carefully watch for it. We want them to love each other and be for each other when they become adults. How they learn to inter- act in their toddler, elementary, and teenage years will play directly into how they see each other as they become adults. The relational baggage they pack is intimately connected to the *comparison bags* that we will address in chapter five. The bottom line is this: we have to be aware that the sibling Relational Bag can be a big one.

## Relationships With Friends

I had a lot of friends in high school. I wasn't the most popular kid on campus, but since I played on the football team and was a part of student government, I knew a lot of people. I didn't have a ton of close relationships, but there were a few guys that I knew I could count on. My best friend today is a guy I met in ninth grade. He was a part of a crew that helped me first understand what it means to have a relationship with God, and I will forever be grateful to him. We were in many classes together, played sports together, hung out on the weekends and, in my view, were almost in the "best friend" category. The graduation week of our senior year was a lot of fun. We goofed off at school all week, had the annual senior picnic, and dealt with all the things that lead up to the big ceremony. One day, a group of us was in line together for the dreaded graduation practice where we learn how to walk in a line with a partner and sit through a mock service. One of the teachers who was leading the practice told us to pair up to walk in together. Five of us stood there and awkwardly looked around. Two of the guys were clearly best friends and were a natural pairing. That left three: me, my friend, and another guy who we were very close to as well. My friend looked around, moved next to the other guy and said, "Look at us, two sets of brothers" (referring to the four of them). He then looked at me and said, "I don't know what you are. Some kind of cousin or something." I didn't know what to say. Luckily, another good friend was close by and we paired up. I packed a relational bag that day.

Peer relationships are tough. They always have been and always will be. Even when we have a friend to whom we are close, there will be conflict and difficulty that will play into our relationship. We often see our kids face difficult situations with their friends or peers, and they do not know how to navigate the pain. They typically stuff it deep down inside and hope it will go away. It usually doesn't.

As parents, we need to recognize that every day offers the potential for our kids to pack a Relational Bag through their interactions with their peers. We will obviously never be able to know about every interaction they have and help them process how they are relating to their friends, but we do need to do our best to pay attention to what is happening to our kids because of their relationships with their friends. Is there tension? Is there drama? Is there frustration? As they navigate their friendships, are they learning how to deal with conflict in a healthy way, or are they simply packing a bag and wondering whether or not they can ever have any real friends? I am in no way suggesting that we need to be *helicopter parents* and step in to solve problems for our kids. I've heard stories of teenage couples breaking up and parents wanting to "call a meeting" to mediate. Our kids need to learn how to deal with peer relationships in healthy ways, and they need us to help them in this process. We need to pay attention to their hearts and do what we can to keep them from packing bags that will hinder them having healthy relationships in the future.

## The Burden of the Bag:
## What Happens if the Relational Bag Gets Packed?

I do not pretend to know exactly what will happen if our kids pack these bags, and I know there are people with a lot more knowledge and wisdom than I have who have taught and written about the consequences of carrying long-term baggage. But, based on what I have heard and seen over the years, I can give us a small snapshot of the ramifications of packing relational bags. If our kids pack relational bags, they could:

- Have a hard time trusting people—When relationships are strained and kids wonder if those who are seemingly closest to them "have their backs," they struggle to open up and be real with anyone.
- Question whether they want to have a family—When a child's family experience has been one of relational struggle, pain, and disappointment, he or she might wonder if it's all worth it and be unsure of the possibility of having a healthy family themselves.

- Have a hard time building close friendships—When childhood experiences consist of a string of failed friendships, people tend to struggle in their adult friendships and have a hard time developing true community.

- Struggle with intimacy—When they have never been able to get close to anyone emotionally, they tend to hold back in their key relationships and struggle to let anyone in. This plays into their sexual lives with their spouse.

- Tend to be more isolated—When they feel like they are failures in most of their relationships, they tend to want to become more of a loner. It's just easier.

## Lightening the Load:
## Ways to Prevent Our Kids Packing the Relational Bag

There is no doubt that everything in life revolves around relationships, and relationships can be tough. As parents, we can learn to be proactive and fight against our kids packing relational bags.

### *Model healthy relationships in the home.*

Kids learn a lot of what they know about relationships from the home. If you are married, do everything you can to have a healthy relationship with your spouse. If you are divorced, do your best to honor your former spouse (especially in front of your kids). You'll be amazed at the message this will send. If you are not married and are dating, do everything you can to model healthy relationships and have proper boundaries. Our kids are watching, and these relationships will have more of an influence on them than we will ever know.

As adults, do your best to have healthy relationships with your parents and siblings. If your kids know you have a bad relationship with your mom or dad or brother or sister and they see you fighting with them or talking bad about them, you are planting the seed that they might not be able to have a good relationship with their immediate family (you) when they become adults. Honor and lift up your parents and siblings as best you can. After all, that's what you are asking your kids to do!

When it comes to your friends, choose good ones! Your kids can pick up on the influence your friends are having on you, good or bad. If we tell our kids they need to be surrounding themselves with positive influences, we need to do the same. We also need to model what it means to be in a healthy conflict with a friend. If we talk badly about our friends, guess what our kids are likely to do? Again, our kids are getting their cues on how to navigate relationships mostly from us. Let's show them what it means to be a good friend.

### *Give them time and attention.*

Kids of all ages want our time. Their words and body language may sometimes say otherwise, but they crave healthy relationships with us, and that takes time. In a culture where we are always busy and forever distracted, we have to make quality time with our families (and particularly with our kids) a real priority.

In giving our kids time, we have to remember they are smart and observant, and they know when time doesn't equal attention. One night while we were at the table eating dinner, I felt compelled to check something that was buzzing on my phone. My son, using a quote from a recent ad campaign, said, "Dad, device-free dinner?" Simply being in the same physical space doesn't mean that I am truly present with others in that same space. If I want my kids to believe I am really there for them and not take steps toward packing a relational bag, I need to step away from technology and put my full attention on them. If I don't, they will notice.

As we navigate this principle, we may have to give them time on their time. If you haven't heard, kids are busy. One day when my daughter got home from soccer practice, she asked me to play a card game with her. I was finishing up something for work, and we were soon to be eating dinner. I had a choice to make. She had the time and was asking me for mine. Thinking about this principle, I walked away from the computer and into a game of Crazy 8s. I was glad I did.

When my son first got a tablet, he was invited to join a group and play a popular game online. He invited me to join the group. I have absolutely no interest in spending my time in that way, so I was inclined to say a quick, "No thanks." I had recently been working with a co-worker at church on a seminar for parents about navigating technology and social media. In the seminar, we were encouraging parents to "be where your kids are" online. This thought was rumbling around in my head when my son invited me to join in on this game. I could have easily declined and tried to suggest some other ways for us to do something together (things that I like to do!). I reluctantly agreed to join in and asked him to teach me how to play. As we sat on the couch and he worked to get me set up, he talked and talked as the "expert" on the game. Over the next few weeks, this game became a way for us to connect and build our relationship. Often, as parents, we need to step into the world where our kids live and connect on their terms instead of only trying to connect through things we like to do.

Finally, we can often fall into the trap of thinking that the time we spend with our kids in their group activities is good enough. We get them into sports or the arts and go to their games or performances. If we think about it, those activities rarely provide the opportunity for quality time. We're helping them have an experience, but most of that experience is with other adults and their peers, not with us. One young adult in a focus group told me, "My parents did everything they could to provide for me. I played four sports and did so much, but we never really had quality time."

### *Offer grace and forgiveness.*

You would not believe the number of young adults who have packed a relational bag because they never felt like their parents gave them any grace. I know what you're thinking: "I give them grace all the time!" It's true, we may give our kids grace upon grace as they grow up. They are simply not mature enough to see it. They don't know how many times we've washed the dishes they forgot to wash or put away their shoes or defended their actions. They don't have the eyes to see or minds to comprehend what we as parents sacrifice for them. Once they are in their young adult years, they have already told themselves a story that is hard to rewind. We often fall into a non-stop cycle of pointing out what they have done wrong or how they haven't lived up to our expectations and they feel the weight of this pressure. I'm certainly not advocating for allowing our kids to get away with being lazy, disrespectful, and entitled. I want my kids to learn responsibility and to take care of things that they need to take care of (more about that in a later chapter). Things have to get done, and they have to do them. However, when we value rules and expectations over the relationship, they feel it deeply. I want a healthy relationship with my kids, and extending grace often paves the way for that kind of relationship to exist.

In those times where our kids have messed up and made poor decisions, we have to remember we may be their only advocates. They already feel isolated and ashamed about what they have done, and they need us more than ever. When they feel like the world is against them, they have to know we are for them. Even when we are disappointed, we may need to hold back in expressing that disappointment to strengthen the relationship and help them process what they have done. Kids need to know we will be there for them no matter what, that they are forgiven, and our love is not conditional.

***Display humility and say, "I'm sorry!"***

Are you aware that, as a parent, you are sometimes in the wrong? Shocking, I know. But all kidding aside, our kids need to know we aren't always right and we sometimes need to ask for their forgiveness. In a world that projects a need for perfection, our kids need to know it's OK to be wrong and make mistakes. I often need to ask God for forgiveness for my words, thoughts, and actions. When in the wrong, I need to model asking for forgiveness from my kids.

Years ago, I heard about a great concept. After any kind of conflict or argument with my kids, I want to do whatever I can to restore the relationship. In other words, I don't want to let the relational distance remain and, even worse, grow. As I've tried to do this over the years, I've learned that it looks different every time, depending on the circumstances and depending on the kid. I need to recognize when I have made mistakes and acknowledge them to my kids. I always want them to know that restoring the relationship is more important than being right. I remember talking with my daughter one night after an argument where I had said a few things I shouldn't have said. I offered a sincere apology and reassured her how much I love her. I'm not sure she's ever hugged me harder than she did that night. Situations like this have played out many times, and I am convinced that my unwillingness to allow the relational distance to remain will pay off in the future.

***Help them build healthy friendships.***

When it comes to building healthy friendships, our kids may sometimes need a little help. I don't think I'm convinced we need to arrange marriages, but I do think we can be strategic and intentional when it comes to whom our kids spend time with. This is easy when they are young, but let's be real: toddler play dates rarely lead to real, deep relationships. As our kids get older, it is harder and harder to monitor and influence whom they have as friends, but it's not impossible.

Our son was thirteen. Several years earlier we had moved to a new town, and although we had been there for a few years and he had a fair number of friends from school, they still weren't the type of "go-to" friends he knew he could always rely on and hang out with. I was just getting to know a family in our town who had a son our son's age. This kid joined our church for our annual summer camp, and I was really impressed with him during that week. When we arrived back at church at the end of the week, I sought out this young man's mom as she picked him up. I told her how impressed I was with her son and that it would be great if the two boys could hang out sometime. I told her, in front of her son, that he was the kind of kid I wanted my son hanging out with. I thought (and hoped) they would get along great. A few days later, the mom reached out to us wondering if we could set up a time for them to hang out. That's right. I organized a playdate for my thirteen-year-old, and it worked.

As parents, we can dial certain people in and out of the lives of our kids. It may take a lot of work and effort, and our kids may sometimes resist, but it's worth it. Pay attention to whom your kids are hanging out with. Early in my ministry, I heard pastor Andy Stanley talk to a group of high school students and share a phrase that has stuck with me for almost three decades. He said, "Your friends will determine the quality and direction of your life."[1] I have probably used that quote hundreds and hundreds of times over the years as I have talked to teens. This principle applies to kids, teens, college students, and adults!

Scripture says it this way: "Walk with the wise and become wise, for a companion of fools suffers harm" (Proverbs 13:20). I want my kids to become wise, go in the right direction, and have quality lives. Their friends will have a lot to do with this, and there are times when I need to help steer them in the right direction.

### Don't compare kids.

We'll learn much more about this later in the chapter on the Comparison Bag. For now, we simply need to do everything we can not to compare our kids to one another, their peers, or anyone else in the world.

Do everything you can to teach your kids to be for one another. Teach them to cheer for each other and celebrate the successes of their siblings. At an early age, teach your kids to pray for each other and ask God to be with their brothers and sisters. Remember there is a natural relational divide that can exist between siblings, so we should do everything we can to help them foster healthy relationships with one another.

### Take the time to just talk.

In a world where we feel like we always have to be efficient and get things done, we can sometimes struggle with seemingly wasting time. Small talk about nothing with our kids can drive us crazy (at least it can me), but we have to learn to talk about anything so we can talk about everything (a concept our pastor talks about often). When we can get into the habit of having conversations with our kids all the time, we set the stage for the big conversations that will come down the road. We have to build a relationship where our kids will share things with us about their thoughts, their dreams, their friendships, and their struggles. If talking to mom and/or dad is not a normal part of their lives by the time they are in their teenage years, it may be hard for them to learn to share intimate details of their lives. Don't fall into the trap of always trying to solve life's problems for them. Just be there for them and listen.

If you have teenagers and you feel like you have missed the boat in building relationships that foster real conversations about real issues, don't give up. It's never too late to strengthen a bond and create a safe place for teens to talk. Deep down our kids long to have a real connection with us where they can trust us and share their hearts. You may not get the results you want overnight, but you can make progress.

### *Be the adult (emotionally).*

So many kids and young adults are incredibly disappointed in their parents' ability to consistently "be the adult." One college student said, "Unfortunately parents aren't relationally mature." It seemed as if she was talking about not only her own parents but her friends' parents as well. As adults, we must work hard not to slip into the immature drama that can so deeply plague relationships. Kids are looking for stability in so many ways, and we have the opportunity to provide the solid foundation they desperately seek. I can remember being told to "act your age" by adults who could not do the same.

Do everything you can to stay away from petty squabbles, arguments, and disagreements. This might be overall good life advice. If you do find yourself getting reeled into such situations, make sure your kids don't get pulled in behind you and do everything you can to shield them from even knowing about them. We want to be authentic with our kids, but there may be times when not knowing may be better for them in the long run.

If we can model what it means to be emotionally stable and healthy, maybe our kids will have the chance to do the same. We can give them confidence in their relationships with us as well as build up their abilities to work through the many struggles and situations that will come their way. If they see us putting our faith and trust in God while demonstrating a maturity that comes from Him, they just might believe they can live the same way.

## Wrapping up the Relational Bag

As I started this project, I quickly learned that the baggage that comes with relationships is huge. I'm pretty sure I already knew this, but I might not have been willing to acknowledge how big it actually is. As adults, we can all point to strained and broken relationships in our lives that have impacted us for years and years. If we know that relationships are central to our very beings, and if we want our kids to experience life to the full, we have to pay attention to the relational bags they are packing. I remember years ago going through an exercise where I identified what I wanted most out of life. This exercise was prompted by reading Philippians 4:7, which encourages us to offer our requests to God and says if we do, "the peace of God, which transcends all understanding, will guard your hearts and your minds in Christ Jesus."

I remember thinking, "That's what I want!" I want peace. I first and foremost want peace with God, and secondly, I want peace with others. I want relational health, free of the baggage that can hold me down.

Our kids want that, too. They want to live their lives free of relational baggage with you as their parent. They want a solid relationship with you, and they want to know they can count on you no matter what. They want a life free of baggage with their brothers and sisters. They long to be close to their siblings and be "for" one another. They want to feel connected with their friends, even as these relationships go up and down over the years. As the relational baggage

34

piles up, our kids don't always know why or how these bags are getting packed. As their parents, we have to help them lighten the load.

## *Reflection Questions*

How would you evaluate your current relationship with your kids? (Be honest!) What are some practical things you can do to build or strengthen your relationship?

What are your child's interests? How can you engage in their interests with them? Plan a parent/child date. Ask your children what they want to do rather than coming up with it on your own.

If you have more than one child, how would you describe the relationships your kids have with each other? What are some things you can do to help your kids strengthen their relationships with one another?

Sometimes one of your children may need more of your attention than others. In these seasons, how can you make sure your other kids don't feel neglected?

Often in a family a parent can relate better to one child than another. Can you think of any ways you may be unwittingly showing favoritism or what could be perceived as favoritism by another child? Ask a spouse or close friend if they see any favoritism or patterns that may not be healthy.

How are you modeling healthy relationships to your kids? Are there things you need to improve or components of any relationships that need to be handled in private?

Is it difficult for you to admit you are wrong and apologize to your child? Why or why not?

How can you determine when your children need discipline and when they need grace? What would it look like to offer both at the same time?

Does your child have any relationships you are concerned about? What are your concerns? What are ways you could address these concerns with your child?

**Endnotes**

1 Andy Stanley and Stuart Hall, *Max Q Student Journal*, Howard Books, 2004, 102.

*Chapter Three*

# The Performance Bag

*"The lie I sometimes feel is that I am what I accomplish."—young adult*

Can you hear the voices? I know you can. They're constant. They're loud. And, for most kids, they're overwhelming. Take a trip to a youth soccer game. When you get there, just listen. Don't talk, just listen. I can remember the first time I noticed this. I had heard and read about these voices, but it was quite a different thing to experience them myself. Our daughter had just started playing soccer in our new town and my wife and I were settled into our lawn chairs on a sunny Saturday afternoon. The girls went through their warmups, and we were exchanging pleasantries with some of the other parents. All was calm, and then something crazy happened. The game started and you would have thought we were in the World Cup. The passion was high, the tension thick, and the pressure was on. And it was all coming from the parents.

As the game progressed, the voices were pretty much non-stop. "Get to the ball!" "Mark that girl!" "She's open, pass it!" I could hear the coach trying to direct the girls from his side of the field, but the voices on our side mostly drowned out his attempt to do his job. I loved hearing one ten-year-old sum up what I believe a lot of the other girls were probably thinking when she turned and yelled, "Mom, stop talking to me. You're not my coach!"

Kids today are growing up packing a Performance Bag that is enormous. They feel like they have to perform everywhere they go, and their sense of worth is tied to their achievements. In one of our focus groups, a young adult shared, "Everything that is an output from a young person is tied to some sort of approval."

Did you catch that? Kids today are being made to feel they have to *perform* in order to gain approval. They have to produce in order to be loved. This bag is so big and has so much poured into it that it has four compartments. It starts being packed in the home with family and continues with that first experience in sports, in those first days in the classroom, and in daily interactions with peers. We were once at a school function where an administrator praised a certain group of students and proclaimed they had "allowed their achievements to become simply a part of who they are." So, my performance and my achievements are a part of my identity?

Kids today have few places in life where they feel like they *don't* have to perform. Life is simply one constant competition. They know they are being evaluated in almost every conversation and every interaction. Because of its several layers, the Performance Bag is ever-present and getting heavier each day. In almost every focus group, college students and young adults quickly identified the pressure to perform as one of the heaviest burdens they carry. In one focus group we facilitated, a young lady described it this way: "I went to a competitive high school, and there was a tremendous pressure to perform. I felt that at home, too. I'm the oldest and, as the older sibling, I was disciplined more. There were higher expectations for me, and I had to set the bar for my sisters." A young man in the group chimed in, "I had pressure as the youngest. I had to live up to my brother." A third guy said, "Oh, as an only child I had a tremendous amount of pressure to perform. All eyes were on me!" So, three college students who were all in the same focus group but all from different family structures have felt this enormous pressure to perform—for years. I was recently talking to a mom of an 11th grader who was on the brink of tears talking about how this pressure was tearing her son apart.

Now, I know what you might be thinking. Here comes the "pastor talk" about how performance is not important and how we should be thinking on a higher plane. Well, that's partially true. As a former athlete, long-time high school football coach, and an all-around competitive guy, I am all about some performance. As a dad, I certainly want to encourage my kids to perform to the best of their abilities and reach for the stars. For most of us, there is real tension with this bag. You might ask, "What's wrong with pushing my kids to perform? They are going to have to learn how to perform sooner or later. You have to perform to survive in the world!" On most levels, I agree.

The question is, "At what cost?" I know a lot of stories of kids who were pushed and pushed to perform in sports and walked away from it all early in high school because they were tired of the pressure. I have known college students who were pressured to perform academically while in high school so they could get into the *right* school, only to hate that school once they arrived. If you simply listen to young adults, you can hear them asking whether the sacrifice, damaged relationships, and lost time was worth it. I think we need to start asking ourselves, "What does success look like for our kids as they grow up?" If we play into the idea that success equals performance, then we are contributing to our kids packing some huge bags in their lives that will go far beyond what they accomplish in life.

One young adult said, "We equate performance with being a good person." Our kids are measuring where they stack up morally based on how they perform!

But I believe there *is* a way we can help our kids reach their potential while keeping them from packing the performance bag. I want my kids to do *their* best, not feel the pressure to be *the* best at everything they do. There's a big difference between the two. In a world where very few kids are going to be *the* best, what does that mean for the rest of the crowd? I can tell you for sure that most kids and young adults today are crumbling under the pressure to perform in several ways:

- Performance in school.
- Performance in sports.
- Performance with peers and friends.
- Performance with family.

As parents, we aren't the only ones making deposits into the Performance Bag, but one young adult did put it this way: "You kind of become a product or a project of your parents instead of a child of your parents."

## *Performance in School*

When it comes to stressing about school, my wife and I might be as low-key as they come. Don't get me wrong, we want our kids to get their work done and do their best. We were good students, and we value education. We're also the parents that will pull our kids out of school the week after spring break to take a ski trip out west with friends.

As our kids have gone through elementary and middle school, we have not exerted a ton of academic pressure. My wife has definitely carried the majority of the load when it comes to navigating our kids' education but, on the whole, our house has been relatively pressure-free when it comes to performing in school. No cash for good grades and no punishment for bad ones.

You can imagine our surprise when, in the fall of her 6th grade year, our daughter started proclaiming, "I can't get a B!" (implying she had to get all A's). This was no passing emotion about one particular test or project; it was a prevailing wind about her life at school. This mindset came with angst, fear, and plenty of drama. We tried to lovingly tell her that we were proud of her no matter what, as long as she did her best. We had been telling her that for years, and for some reason, it had not settled into her psyche.

I started to wonder where this pressure was coming from. Was it teachers? Was it her peers? Was it the overall culture at school? Is it just her personality? A bag was being packed that, if left unchecked, could crush her as she entered high school and college. Imagine the pressure that comes with "I can't get a B!" I was right at the beginning of the "Bags" project during this season and, for some reason, this was the first time I realized that others had the ability to pack these bags for my kids. Although this burden to perform in school wasn't coming from us, it was coming from somewhere. The influences from outside our home were taking over and our little girl was developing a mindset that we needed to change.

The school performance bag is heavy. Most kids today are feeling *overwhelming* pressure when it comes to school, and they are packing a bag that says, "You have to perform or you're just not good enough." We all recognize that the way our kids perform in school has a real impact on their future. Their school performance can dictate if they can further their education in college, and it determines where they can get into school. It is important!

But how important? Is it so important they should feel such immense pressure to perform that it crushes them? Is their performance in school so important that it should consume their middle and high school years and rob them of experiences they can never get back? Is the long-term benefit of getting that extra three-tenths of the grade point average worth the lost years that so quickly fade away? Is it so important that we're okay with our kids believing they are not "good enough" if they don't get the best grades or get into the right college? Is the anxiety worth it? These are questions we as parents have to answer.

## *Performance in Sports*

Like I mentioned earlier, I have coached high school football for twenty years. When I started, I was working full-time as a youth pastor at a local church and was invited to coach at the high school where I played. Because of these years of experience, I know a fair amount about coaching youth football. When my son was in 4th grade, we signed up to play Pop Warner youth football. I had since retired from coaching, and I had no intentions of jumping back in. I was planning on enjoying the games from the stands. On the first day of practice, the head coach held an impromptu parent meeting where he explained there were too many boys for one team, so they would be splitting into two. If there was anyone who had any coaching experience, they could use the help. I knew I had to do it.

Over the next week, I did all the paperwork and made my way onto the field. It was obvious this group of dads had been coaching together for a few years and had a real program in place. After a week or so, we began to talk about how to split the teams, and I knew I was in trouble. The plan was to have an "A" team and a "B" team with the older, stronger, better kids all together on the "A" team. My son was on the younger, smaller side and was clearly slated for the "B" team. Oh, and did I mention that I was the only dad who answered the call to help coach? Soon they approached me about being the head coach of the "B" team.

Now, I know the "A" and "B" approach is common in a lot of youth sports. It can work. In football, though, it's an awful idea, especially in our situation where we would be the only "B" team in the league playing against all "A" teams. In football, smaller, younger kids don't just lose by *a lot*; they get hurt, and I knew it. As I challenged these dads about the plan, it was clear they weren't going to budge. One night during a break I was pushing us to reconsider the plan, and one of the dads said, "Come on man, we have to get these kids to Disney!"

Disney? I thought we were playing football, not planning a vacation. Oh, but I learned. Disney is where the Pop Warner World Championship of All Things Youth Football happens (I made that name up). You see, the rival team across town had gotten to go to Disney a few years earlier, and we just had to push these kids to match that. As the weeks went on these coaches pushed and pushed these 4th and 5th graders to near exhaustion. One night during a break in practice I said, "You know these kids still play with Legos, right?" They thought it was *pastor talk*.

There are countless stories in youth sports where our kids feel the pressure to perform and are packing some giant bags. Here are a few

examples: While at one soccer tournament where we were beating a team we had lost to before, one mom yelled to the 11-year-olds on the other team, "Payback sucks!" In a middle school football game, a dad yelled at his 8th-grade son, "If you're not going to hit someone, then take yourself out of the game." You could see the kid drop his head and pack a bag. That kid hasn't played football since the end of that season. At another game, a dad was talking to his linebacker son during halftime and said (in a pretty loud voice), "Tear their *******
heads off!" Did I mention this was middle school football?

I heard a TEDx talk recently that rocked my world. John O'Sullivan is a former college athlete and college coach, and he leads the "Changing the Game Project." In his talk about "Changing the Game in Youth Sports,"[1] he shared some powerful truths. Did you know that seven out of ten kids who play youth sports quit by the age of 13? They do it because of the toll the pressure to perform takes on them. John says, "When it comes to youth sports, lots of kids end up with physical and emotional scars that last a lifetime." He's talking about bags!

If you had to guess, what would you say that kids identify as one of the things they dread the most about youth sports? I would think it was the conditioning, practice, or something to do with the sacrifices they have to make. Nope. Ready for this? It's the ride home. It's the time when they get into the car with us and they have to listen to everything they could have done better. They are coming off the excitement of a win, the pain of a loss, or the simple joy of getting to play a game they love. We are looking at it as another time to correct and direct. I could write on and on about the performance bags kids are packing in youth sports, but my guess is you can see it.

## Performance With Peers and Friends

As I walk around our church's youth room most every week, I am often reminded of my middle school and high school days. I remember the awkward times of trying to figure out which circle to join and what words to say. I remember worrying about what I was wearing and what people thought of me. I remember trying to figure out where I belonged and how I fit in. It was hard work!

I watched this teenage dilemma play out a few years ago as we attended an event for our 14-year-old son. As we left home, he didn't seem too excited to go. His best friend was not going to make it, and I knew he only had one other guy he connected with who would be there. When we arrived and went to sit down, he went to a table with some of the guys. We were in the cafeteria seated at thin, long tables. As we started dinner, I watched my son essentially get "shut out" of the conversation at his table. His seat was at the end of the group, and the guy next to him turned his body to face the other kids and away from my son. As the conversation went on, my son ate by himself as the crew carried on and laughed. Finally, after about fifteen minutes, my son grabbed his plate and moved from one side of the line of seats (around about six guys) to the other where he could have a better entry into the conversation.

Kids today have to perform socially just like we did. They have to learn how to navigate new and old friends. They have to discern what they can and can't say, what they should and shouldn't wear, where they should and shouldn't go, and which groups they have to lobby to join. On the surface, things look just like they did years (and decades) ago. However, as parents, we need not fall into the trap of thinking that growing up today is just like it was "back in the day" when we were going through our elementary and teenage years. Sure, some things remain the same, but our world today (and particularly their world) is so drastically different that it's almost another game altogether. I recently heard it described this way: years ago, the school lunchroom was the main place where we had to work hard to perform. I can remember having to rush from class to get my food so I could get in the right spot at the right table. Once at the table, I had to make sure I was relevant in the conversation and perform for my friends. I had to do this in the classroom, on the court, on the field, and at parties with friends. But when I got home and away from my peers, I could relax. I could take a break from being in the "performance mode" that kept me in the social game. I had a place to retreat.

We all know what the game-changer is for our kids. It's the technology they carry in their hands at almost every waking moment. In today's world, not only do our kids have to perform socially at school (in the lunchroom), but they also have to perform socially online, which means *all the time*. The lunchroom hasn't just moved—it's gotten infinitely bigger!

As parents, we have to understand that if our kids are using social media, they live in a world of non-stop comparison, and they think they *have* to perform socially. Their pictures have to be staged, edited, and altered to look like they are experiencing their best lives, and everything is amazing. While many of us used to have to *one-up* each other verbally only when we were together, kids today have to not only top their friends online, but they feel the pressure to have to top their last performance by getting more *likes* than their previous post. It's never-ending. One college student said it this way: "We live in a world where you have your own personal brand. You have to live up to what your brand is and non-stop worry about your image."

So, we are now raising a generation of kids who feel the social pressure to build and cultivate their own brand. They have to spend time, effort, brain power, and emotions performing socially, and they have to do it all the time.

## Performance With Family

When I was growing up, I loved getting together with extended family. Most of our gatherings happened at my grandmother's house, and they were loads of fun. As one of the youngest cousins, I remember having to sit at the "kids' table" during meals and anticipating the time when I could graduate up. These were fun times, and I always looked forward to them.

Now that I'm older, I still get excited about these kinds of gatherings. Maybe I have just been naïve for a long time, but I am relatively shocked at the number of adults who dread the thought of several days with their extended families. I hear stories of the passive-aggressive mother-in-law or the overbearing brother. People worry about how their kids will behave and how they will be perceived as parents. It often seems as if adults who have seemingly moved on to their own lives get drawn back into old patterns that tear them down. We are still holding some sort of bags.

Many people grow up feeling like they have to perform in their families. They have to somehow earn the love of those they are supposed to be closest to. This so intimately ties in with the pressure to perform everywhere else in life. We seem to feel like we have to live up to the standards of others in order to be accepted. We start life learning that performing for our parents makes them happy and life better for us. We try to navigate relationships with our siblings by either trying to out-perform them or reserving ourselves to the fact that we will never measure up. Neither outcome is ideal.

As we talked about family, relationships, and performance with one focus group, a young adult said, "I was always afraid in my performance to disappoint my parents, and I'm still waiting for their approval." So many people live by looking at their lives through this lens.

### The Burden of the Bag:
### What Happens if the Performance Bag Gets Packed?

Performance baggage is some of the heaviest we carry and can have a tremendous impact on people as they move into adulthood. If our kids pack performance bags, they could:

- Define themselves based on how well they do (or do not) perform—When kids believe they are the sum of their accomplishments, they develop an identity based on what they perceive they can or cannot do.

- Question their worth—When your life revolves around your performance, it is easy to question your worth, even when you are able to perform.

- Struggle relationally with those who exert pressure—When teachers, coaches, and parents pour on the relentless pressure, kids can easily distance themselves relationally when they feel like acceptance is based on performance.

- Develop a pattern of constant competition—When the need to perform is ever-present, kids can develop a mindset that they are always competing with those around them.

- Shrink back and lose self-confidence—When the expectation to perform leads to the need to be "the best," kids can emotionally crumble or shut down.

- Live with non-stop pressure and anxiety—When kids feel a constant pressure to perform and don't have the tools to deal with the emotions, anxiety and depression can quickly take hold.

## Lightening the Load:
## Fighting the Performance Bag

As we have seen and we know, the pressure to perform can consume our kids. We have the opportunity to do a few things to help alleviate this pressure.

***Remind them you love them, and their identity is not rooted in their performance.***

Every day we have the opportunity to steer our kids away from packing the performance bag and help them understand that the foundation of their lives does not have to stand on how well they perform. I believe our kids need to hear us tell them how much we love them over and over again. It almost needs to rise to the level where they roll their eyes and say, "I know, you love me."

When our kids were young, we started to try to plant this truth into their hearts. Most nights when they would go to bed, I would ask them "Did you know…?" and then I would list off four things. I started with, "Number one: Did you know your mom and I and your brother/sister love you with all of our hearts!" I then added, "Number two: Did you know that as much as we love you, God loves you more!" I would finish with the other two "Did you knows?" I repeated this most nights for several years. (We eventually added numbers 5-8 and 9-12). With that kind of repetition, they got to a point where they could speak it with me. None of the questions were tied to performance on their part but on an unconditional love that comes from their earthly parents, their sibling, and their heavenly

Father. We hope and pray these truths are written on their hearts and help to guide who they are.

Our kids need not to only *hear* this from us, but they need to *feel* it from us, too. They need to know that God loves them no matter what they do or don't do in life. They need to know that our love is not conditional and, most importantly, not based on their performance in any area of life. We love them because of who they are, and the same is true of God. Their identities come from who He has created them to be, not in the sum of their accomplishments and performance.

### *Reduce the pressure in your home.*

As parents, we have the opportunity to either increase or reduce the pressure at home. I suggest reducing the pressure. I recommend turning down the heat. Allow your home to be a place of refuge and rest for your kids, not another pressure-cooker of performance. Figure out how you can appropriately push and prod your kids so they can accomplish their goals. Notice, I said *their* goals, not yours. This may be one of the hardest things for us as parents to do.

Encourage them to be the best they can be and do the best they can do. There is definitely tension around what to do when you know they're *not* being the best they can be and they're *not* doing the best they can do. I would suggest loving them anyway and make sure they know it. Encourage them and help them as they work through whatever is in front of them. But don't forget that you can't own it and let your desire for them to perform override their desires to be successful. If we do, we will create an environment at home that will contribute to packing the performance bag.

### *Don't compare.*

I know we already addressed some of this in the Relationship Bag, but I can't tell you how many times I've heard young adults struggle with the fact that they live in a world of non-stop comparison. They feel it in school, they feel it in their activities, they feel it online, and they feel it at home. Almost every day I hear one of my kids say something like, "Why doesn't he have to help?" or "How come she gets to do that?" The comparison seems to be natural. Since they are already comparing themselves to everyone else, we should work hard not to pile on.

For some reason, we often think that comparison will work as a tool to motivate our kids. If we're honest, sometimes it does. But just because something might work doesn't that it's healthy and we should do it. I would encourage you to stop comparing your kids. Don't compare them to each other, don't compare them to their peers, and don't compare them to the rest of the world. They already know where they stack up against others, and any comparisons we make further pushes them to believe they have to perform better than someone else in order to gain our love and approval.

### *Be aware of the social pressure.*

We've already touched on the reality of the social pressures our kids face, and I hope you are convinced this pressure is real and has the potential to pack some huge bags. Please do not minimize the layers of social pressure that exist, and do not ignore the ramifications of it all. I could tell you story after story of kids and teens who have been crushed under the pressure and weight of having to perform socially. Kids are asking, "Am I *ever* good enough?" and much of their answer to that question comes from how they feel socially.

If your kids are on social media platforms, I would suggest doing something I heard a few years ago and mentioned earlier in the book: be where they are. Join whatever social network they choose to be a part of and follow them. As you follow, pay attention to the things they post and the reactions those posts get. You can learn a lot about your children and their world from what you see them share and how their friends react. When you see something that raises your curiosity, ask them about it and have a conversation, knowing that you may not get all of the answers you are looking for in one conversation. Remember this is a marathon, not a sprint, and there can be more talks along the way. Be aware that teens may create fake accounts that you are not aware of in order to communicate with their friends free of the "adult world." If your kids push back on you being in their digital worlds, stand your ground, and let them know your presence is non-negotiable.

I was recently talking to a youth leader about the world kids are growing up in and he said, "They live in a world that isn't real. It's essentially a fake space." Because of this, they have real trouble moving back and forth between what is real and what is fake. They need help to know what is appropriate and acceptable. They will easily post something they might never say to someone in person. As parents, we have the opportunity (and responsibility) to help our kids navigate their social landscapes, and it all starts with being aware of their social world.

***Praise them for their godly qualities (not their performance).***
It was basketball season, and I was working on this part of the project. Both my son and my daughter were on teams, and we had games almost every weekend. When we got in the car after a game, I decided that instead of pointing out how great it was that they scored this many points or got that many steals, I would say something like this: "I loved it when you helped that kid who fell get up off the floor." I looked for opportunities to say, "You really were encouraging to your teammates during that part of the game." I decided to praise them for the godly qualities I saw them display and not for how well they performed. I wanted to coach character.

I want my kids to develop as athletes, musicians, artists, students, and friends. But more than that, I hope to help them develop as followers of Jesus who reflect the image of God to the world around them. I have the opportunity to point them in that direction, and part of the way I can do that is to praise them for the times I see them displaying the qualities I pray they embrace. If we want to steer our kids away from packing a worldly performance bag and push them toward being "imitators of God" (Ephesians 5:1), then we need to make sure we are praising them for the things we want to see continue to grow in their lives.

Look for opportunities to catch your kids not just doing something *good*, but train yourself to see them exhibiting qualities that flow from their Creator. Help them see when God is working through them in the way they show kindness, generosity, patience, or self-control. Reinforce the Fruit of the Spirit (Galatians 5:22-23) and encourage your kids when they display these qualities in their daily lives. Offer them frequent verbal encouragement in the direction you want them to go, and don't reserve your praise for only when they perform. Praise them for the way you see God at work in them and through them.

## Wrapping up the Performance Bag

As I started this project, I inherently knew that the Performance Bag was a big one. I'm not sure I understood just how heavy this bag is for people and how long we carry it around. There are so many layers to the pressure to perform, and our kids have no way to process the weight they feel. In focus group after focus group, I heard people talk about the pressure to perform. One young adult defined performance as "the pressure to live up to some standard in order to be accepted or be loved. The pressure to be perfect."

The Performance Bag often starts with the expectations that our culture (and we as parents) pile on our kids far earlier than they are ready to handle. The pressure to meet the requirements placed upon them steals away the joy of life and puts our kids in an incredibly difficult place emotionally. They see the way the adults around them react when they fail to meet the expectations, and they are driven to struggle with their ability to perform. As adults, we need to know that our kids are often wrecked when they feel like they don't add up to the mound of expectations placed upon them. As childhood and teenage anxiety go up in our culture, parents need to do everything we can to fight this trend.

In John O'Sullivan's TEDx Talk, he encourages parents to say this after a game: "I really enjoy watching you play." That's it. No commentary. No play-by-play evaluation. No criticism. What if, after a game or a match or a recital or a project, we tried *not* to correct our kids for *anything* they could have done better? What would happen in the hearts of our kids if we just encouraged them and let them know what a joy it is for us, as their parents and biggest fans, and that we simply love watching them do what they love to do, no matter how good they are?

We have the opportunity to change the tide. We have the power as the primary leaders in our kids' lives to point them in a different direction. Although the other voices in their lives are loud and demanding, we can help them see there is a different way to live and they are not defined by their abilities to perform. As you will continue to see, these bags are intertwined and often one leads to another. The pressure to perform can quickly push our kids to develop identities based not on who they are created to be, but on what they think they can do. Our desire to drive them to maximize their potential can create a relational distance that is hard to recover. As parents, we have to be aware of the emotional baggage the push to perform is creating, and we have to be willing to fight against the tendency to push them even more than they can handle. We have to be committed to doing everything we can to help them know they are *not* defined by what they do, and they are loved no matter what.

## Reflection Questions

Take some time to reflect on whether you struggle with the pressure to perform in your own life. If you do, how could this have an impact on your kids' view of performance?

How would you describe the atmosphere in your home when it comes to performance? Is there a lot of pressure? Do you see your kids struggling with the pressure to perform? If so, how do you see this playing out in their lives?

What are some ways you can encourage your kids to do *their* best without them feeling the pressure to be *the* best?

What are some godly qualities you see emerging in your children that you can intentionally foster and affirm? Make a list of the qualities for each of your kids.

Are you following your children (and their friends) on their social media platforms to see what they are experiencing?

How do you react when your child falls short?

**Endnotes**

[1] John O'Sullivan, "Changing the Game in Youth Sports." TEDx Talks, March 2014, https://youtu.be/VXw0XGOVQvw.

## Chapter Four

# The Identity Bag

*"Middle and high school are both a slaughter ground for a kid who has no sense of identity."—college student*

I recently met with a mom whose thirteen-year-old daughter is struggling with identity in a big way. The girl had shared with her small group leader at church that she had her first sexual encounter, and she thought she might be pregnant. This girl has several different social media accounts where she portrays a personality that you simply do not see when you meet her in person. She has started to use an e-cigarette because she says it helps to "calm her mind." She struggles with her place in life, and she is desperately trying to figure out who God has created her to be. She has been in church and has a real relationship with God. She says she wants to change and turn away from who she is becoming, she just doesn't know how to do it.

Over the last few decades, the conversion about kids and identity has been rich. Some of the leading voices on this topic have come from the Fuller Youth Institute. In the book *3 Big Questions That Change Every Teenager,* Kara Powell and Brad Griffin talk about the struggle our kids face. "Almost every question young people are asking ultimately finds its genesis in these three big questions:

- Who am I?
- Where do I fit?
- What difference can I make?"[1]

Many leaders and organizations have been encouraging both parents and church leaders to take the time to understand what our kids are experiencing through their adolescent years. When it comes to building their identity, our kids are in a battle and we, as their parents, need to be in the fight *with* them. As kids move out of elementary school and into middle and high school, they will *try on* different versions of themselves in an effort to discern who they are. They sometimes move between multiple identities each day, depending on the situation they are in or the people they are with. This process can be stressful, painful, and confusing, and it can leave teens with some enormous baggage.

One of the first people I heard talk about the importance of identity and the adolescent journey was Dr. Chap Clark. His work at the Fuller Youth Institute and his book *Hurt 2.0* was instrumental not only for me but for so many who are working to help kids and teens grow up with a healthy sense of self. There is so much great research and insight on this topic, and I would encourage you to dive into the resources provided by Dr. Clark as well as those being produced by the current team at Fuller. These resources do a great job of painting the picture of the identity and abandonment struggles kids are facing today. For this chapter, I'll focus on stories I've heard from students and young adults in our focus groups and offer a few practical suggestions on how you can help kids grow up and hopefully avoid some of the Identity Baggage that can weigh them down for years and years.

## *Who Am I?*

I met Sam when he was in elementary school. His dad worked at my church and was one of the pastors who was kind of a mentor to me. Sam was funny, smart, and usually played the *class clown* role almost everywhere he went. I started spending real time with him when he was in middle and high school. He came to youth group every Sunday night, went on camps and mission trips, and quickly became one of my favorite teens. Sam seemed serious about his faith, but I always wondered if he had just adopted his parents' faith instead of developing his own. He was always able to adapt to the situation and fit in with whatever group he was in. You could tell that was important to him.

Sam was active in church for several years, even into his freshmen year in college. As I kept in touch with him, I could tell that he was struggling to figure out his identity. He got into the party scene, didn't pay much attention to his schoolwork, and was starting to drift in a big way. All through this time, he was volunteering in the youth ministry at our church. Asking him to volunteer was a way for me to stay close to him and have influence. After a pretty major moral failure, I decided I had to give him some tough love and tell him he couldn't volunteer anymore. It rocked him and he wasn't sure what to do next. In one of the many conversations I had with him about it all, he told me he just didn't know who he was.

I feel like I've seen this story play out so many times. Kids and teens today don't know who they are, and they don't have a solid foundation to stand on while trying to figure it out. They are bombarded with ideas, images, and possibilities, and they don't have the capacity to sort it all out. One young adult said it this way: "We're forced from a young age to develop our identity in several different layers. We're asked, 'What are you going to be when you grow up?'

so we have to think about work. We have to decide about politics and social issues. We are trying to figure out how we are connected to our family and how we think spiritually. You are often forced to make a stance on things you have no idea about." One college student said, "When you pick an identity, you can feel like you are stuck and there is no way out." Once a kid or teen is labeled by the masses, it can be incredibly hard to overcome what has been put on them. Another student said, "I have so many different boxes that people try to put me in. I feel like if I try to fully go into one box, I get pulled apart on the inside."

So, some kids are moving in and out of different identities while others make decisions that trap them for years and years. This is complicated! "Who am I?" is a huge question to grapple with, and one that can linger for a lifetime. Kids are thrust into a culture that forces them to deal with these questions at an earlier and earlier age, and they cannot sort through it all. I recently heard someone describe it this way: "Kids today are more exposed to the world than ever, but they are not more mature to deal with it all."

Add on the growing confusion and social pressure regarding gender identity, and it is no wonder kids are overwhelmed. So, what do they do? They stuff it all down and pack some enormous bags.

### *Does anyone like or love me?*

As kids grow up and search to find their identity, they are actually searching for *acceptance*. They want to know where they fit in and, more importantly, who they fit in with. In one of our focus groups, the conversation revolved around this idea and one student said, "We have such a desire to fit in. There are so many cliques in society, and you feel like you need to find the right box to fit in. If you don't fit in a particular box, you don't fit in." Someone else said, "Often kids will land in an identity based on who likes them."

60

One of the reasons why kids will pick an identity and stay there is because they feel like they have found their people or their "tribe" as some call it. One student said that adolescents will land "where they feel safe or where they belong—even if they don't like that thing (band, sports, etc.). They stay because they feel safe and accepted." So, safety and acceptance win the day. These are two big things that kids (and I would argue adults) seek from life.

As parents, we need to be aware of this constant search for acceptance and know that this quest impacts almost every area of our kids' lives. It will push them to make decisions they might not normally make. They will put themselves in situations that can hurt them, physically and emotionally. They will say and do things to fit in. They will change the clothes they wear and the music they listen to. In some ways, this process is natural. In other ways, if ignored and left unchecked, it can be incredibly difficult and lead someone to a place they never wanted to be.

### *Am I just the sum of what I have accomplished?*

As I started focusing more of my ministry on helping parents, I heard a story from a young lady at our church. We were planning for a seminar on "Navigating Family, Faith, and Sports" where we were going to talk with parents about how the youth sports culture can dominate our families. This young adult had been an all-star high school athlete who moved into college and continued her success. She was a key member of a division one national championship-winning team, and she had accomplished great things in her career. During her teenage years, she was pushed to work hard, sacrifice, and be the best. She climbed to the top of the athletic mountain, and then she crashed.

In her early 20s, she struggled with her identity. Because she had spent years believing that her accomplishments defined who she was, she was lost when she no longer felt like she was accomplishing big things. She got caught up in the party scene, struggled in relationships, and it took her years to dig out of the depression that had set in. I hear many stories like hers. In one focus group, a college student summed it up well: "As a kid, I felt the pressure to share something that I had achieved (I got an 'A' today. I set a personal record, etc.). I still feel the pressure to share that today. The lie I sometimes feel is that 'I am what I accomplish.'"

"Everything that is an output from a young person is tied to some sort of approval." This observation from a college student that we shared in our last chapter points to the immense pressure kids today feel as they try to build their lives and identity on what they have done. They feel approved when they perform, and this approval shapes how they are building their identity. As parents, we sometimes play into this mentality. We build trophy walls for our kids where we display a bank of things they have accomplished. We have good intentions (usually), and we are trying to celebrate them and what they have accomplished. The problem is that it sometimes leads them to believe that what they have done is who they are.

What happens when all that goes away? What happens when there are no more championships to be won, plays to star in, or awards to be given? How does a young adult process who they are when they have spent all their life striving to accomplish things that have defined them? They start to ask themselves, "Is that all I am?"

### Am I just the sum of my failures?

In the same way youth struggle with defining themselves by their achievements, they can also define themselves by their failures. While many kids may struggle with defining their identity by what they have done (achievements), others struggle with defining their identity by what they have done *wrong*. Some failures may come from simply not being good enough at something, not properly preparing, or from making poor moral choices. Regardless of what caused this perception of falling short, we don't want them to define themselves by their failures or their sin. We don't want their identity to be tied to what they have done—good or bad. I'll talk more about this in the chapter on guilt and shame, but think it is important to bring it to light in this chapter as well.

It's so easy for kids and teens to begin to tell themselves a story of failure. As a volunteer high school football coach, I see it all the time on the field. An athlete will make a mistake, drop their head in frustration or embarrassment, and have a hard time snapping out of it. They will begin to tell themselves that they can't catch the ball, make the block, or perform the task. Unfortunately, we as adults can add fuel to this fire in the way we interact with kids and teens when they are learning to work through overcoming failure. In talking about learning to build an identity, one student said, "Adults have no idea the weight of their words."

"We sometimes find our identity in our baggage, and we believe it's too late to change our story." I heard this comment from a young adult who was admittedly still struggling to find his identity. So many kids, teens, and young adults start down a path that is hard to turn from. In their book, *Hope Lies Ahead: An Encouragement for Prayers of Prodigals From a Family That's Been There,*[2] Geoff and James Banks tell their family's story of a fight for identity. Geoff (a personal friend and co-worker) started down a dark road as a teen and got into some major trouble. Early in the book, Geoff shares about how, when he started to run with the "wrong crowd" and step into substance addiction, he "...chased after my new identity, being fooled into thinking I was someone original."[3] During several years of spiraling down and being in and out of rehab, Geoff found it hard to physically and mentally step away from an identity that he had created. Geoff's story is extreme, and he is a great pastor today, but the principle applies to so many adolescents as they grow up. Identities are forged during the formative years, and the consequences of creating a destructive identity can be crippling.

## The Burden of the Bag:
## What Happens if the Identity Bag Gets Packed?

Identity struggles and issues run deep, and people can struggle with them for a long time. Not all kids deal with the same issues or respond in the same ways, but if our kids pack the identity bag, they could:

- Have a deflated sense of self—When a kid doesn't know who they are, they lose confidence in who God has created them to be and they view themselves as worthless or a failure.

- Question their identity in Christ and struggle to trust God— When a kid, teen, or young adult is not sure they are a child of God, they have a hard time trusting in and following that same God.

- Fall into an identity that leads them away from God—When kids, teens, or young adults don't see a greater purpose in their lives, they may succumb to peer pressure more easily and move even further away from living the life of faith they want to live.

- Have a hard time making real friends—If kids and teens move from identity to identity and group to group, they don't take the time to develop real, authentic friendships and they don't know how to do that in the future.

- Build their identity on a false foundation that cannot last—When anyone builds their foundation on something false that will fade away, they are setting themselves up for an inevitable crash.

- Play the comparison game—When a kid or teen isn't secure in who they are, they tend to compare themselves with their peers to figure out if they measure up, and often feel as if they fall short.

## Lightening the Load: Fighting the Identity Bag

As our kids move through life trying to build their identity, there are a few things we can do to prevent them from packing this bag.

### *Model having and living your identity in Christ.*

"If it's to be, it starts with me!" This popular quote is usually employed to motivate people to take ownership and initiative when it comes to accomplishing things in life. I think we can take this secular, self-motivating challenge and apply it to the way we are leading our kids. We have to understand that who we believe *we are* has a direct impact on who our kids believe *they are*.

If you believe in and follow Jesus, you understand that part of your mission in the world is to share His love with others. When it comes to our kids, one of the ultimate goals is to help them know and embrace their identity in Christ. As we seek to help our kids develop a healthy identity, we first have to understand our own identity. As a follower of Jesus, I need to take time every day to remember who I am and, more importantly, Whose I am. I am a child of God, loved by Him and created to do good works in this world (Ephesians 2:10). As I seek to grasp this each day, I have to do my best to model this to my kids. As parents, we have to know who *we* are in Christ and do our best to live it out every day. If I don't believe I am created and loved by God, it will be hard for my kids to believe the same. One counselor I met with said it this way: "It starts with the parents and their identity. What does the parent identify with? Work? Success? Whatever that is, the kids will follow for sure."

We all know that more is caught than taught. Our kids need to catch us living into our identity in Christ and modeling what that looks like each day.

### *Affirm and teach identity in Christ.*

As we seek to live into our own identity, we have the opportunity to point our kids to their identity in Christ. If they can believe they are who God says they are, they will be on their way to establishing an identity that will give them a solid foundation for life.

Remind your kids that:

- They are a child of God.
- They are fully approved, fully accepted, and fully loved by God.
- They are a beloved child of their parents.
- They are a part of a much bigger plan.
- They were created for a purpose.
- They are uniquely gifted by God.
- They have a bright future.
- God is always with them.

I shared part of this in chapter three, but I think it's worth expanding on here. When our kids were very young, I started trying to instill God's truth into their hearts through a bedtime routine. On many nights I would ask them a series of "Did you know?" questions. It began with, "Did you know your mother, brother/sister, and I love you very much?" It was followed by, "Did you know that as much as we love you, God loves you more?" The third question was, "Did you know you are so very special?" And the fourth was, "Did you know you can do anything with God's help?" After doing this a handful of times, I would begin with "Did you know?" and they would begin to recite the questions with me. When they were younger, I would do this several times a week and it was tons of fun. As they grew older, I would do it less frequently, and instead of reciting the questions with me, they might offer a bit of an eye roll. As the first set of truths took root, we began adding more questions to instill more ideas. We are now up to twelve. Each question is designed to plant in their hearts and minds a truth about who God is and their identity in Him. Even now that they are teenagers, we will occasionally go back to the questions to remind them of the truths of who they are in Christ. I did it just a few days ago with our sophomore daughter, and she could easily recite most of them.

Another way we can teach our kids to grab a hold of the identity they have in God is to affirm what you see in them when it comes to their character. Instead of rewarding your son or daughter for the good grades they earned, celebrate how hard he or she worked to accomplish the goal. Look for times when your child exhibits a fruit of the spirit like kindness, gentleness, or self-control and highlight that. Let's reward our kids (primarily verbally) when we see them embracing and living out the faith and character we are hoping to instill.

### Let them know you love them, and you like them.

All kids (and adults) want to feel loved. We're just wired that way. As parents, we sometimes do a good job telling our kids we love them. They tend to believe it but, as I have mentioned earlier, they can also think it's a part of the parental job description. Years ago, I was encouraged not to only tell my kids that I love them, but to tell them that *I like* them. Deep down they know we love them. I do think they sometimes wonder if we like them. Think about it. Much of your interaction with your kids revolves around what you need them to do—direction and correction. The relationship can seem one-sided and mechanical, especially if there begins to be some emotional distance. Our kids need to believe we want to be around them, we enjoy their company, and they have something to offer the relationship.

When thinking about the culture we are creating in our home, I've begun to ask myself the following questions: When I am correcting my kids, is it because what they are doing is wrong or sinful? Or does it just bug me? Do we subconsciously make rules in our home based on things that annoy us as parents without evaluating whether the action itself is even wrong? If we take that one seriously, it can be a punch to the gut.

Often things that bug us as adults are simply normal child or adolescent behavior. As we correct and discipline our kids for things that aren't inherently wrong, they begin to believe we don't like them and who they are. They question their identity as a valuable member of our family. We need to do everything we can to make sure our kids know we both love them, and we like them. If they feel accepted, liked, and loved by the people who are most important to them, it will relieve a huge amount of pressure and allow them to sort out their identity in a much healthier way.

### Help them build a strong family identity.

Helping a child have a strong sense of belonging in a family can sometimes curb a teen's search for identity in adolescent years. Like most, we have a few traditions that help to make up what it means to be a part of our family. Some of these traditions are just for the four of us, and some of them involve our extended family. All of them help our kids build a stronger bond with our family unit and positively contribute to their identity. We go to church together on Sunday. We have a pancake party with friends and family on Christmas Eve morning. We play a specific game with extended family on Thanksgiving Day. All these things (and more) help our kids develop a strong bond with our family and strengthen their overall identity.

My wife and I recently went through a process at our church to create a "family vision." Okay, maybe we're a little late to the party, but at least we're still trying. During this process, we wrote a mission statement for our family, identified several core family values, and established a few family goals. All of this will hopefully help us all four rally around a common purpose thus strengthening our family identity. To get information about going through a process yourself, visit www.equipandencourage.com.

### *Surround them with others who affirm their identity in Christ.*

Over the last several years, we have been so thankful for a number of people. Geoff, Brett, Taylor, Courtney, Javi, Mary, Nikki, John, Beth, Bill, Woo, and more have all played key roles as our kids have grown and developed. These are people who have given their time and energy to building relationships with our kids, and they have been planting seeds of truth we are praying will take root and blossom. These people are saying the same things we are saying at home and leading our kids into a deeper relationship with God.

We all want people in our kids' lives who are pushing in the same direction we are. If we want our kids to truly embrace their identity in Christ, we need to surround them with people who affirm that identity. Our kids are around people every day that will pull them away from this preferred path. Many friends, coaches, teachers, and co-workers will push them away from their faith and true identity, so we need other voices in their life that will point them toward the abundant life we so desperately want for them.

If you want your kids to embrace their identity in Christ, place people around them to help them do that. Church small groups, Christian clubs at school, and family friends are all great ways to connect your kids to others who will encourage them in their faith. Both my wife and I have intentionally joined groups with our son and daughter so we could put other kids and adults around them to have a positive influence. Making this happen for your kids can take work, but I promise you it is worth it!

### *Extend grace and forgiveness.*

Not only do some of the bags I identify overlap, but the ideas to lighten the load do too. In chapter two on relational bags, I encouraged you to offer grace and forgiveness to strengthen your relationship with your kids. If you don't, your relationship is doomed. Here, the concept of offering grace and forgiveness attacks something else. It lowers the pressure our kids feel to hide who they are from us and allows them to think through their identity *not* based on what they do, but on who they are.

Extending grace and forgiveness also models what God has done for us. Romans 3:23 reminds us that "all have sinned and fall short of the glory of God." That includes us, and our kids know it. We need grace and forgiveness for how we think, how we act, and what we say. As we embrace the grace and forgiveness we need, we can pass that on to our kids.

If we create an atmosphere that does not offer grace and forgiveness, our kids begin to wonder if they even want to follow this God who we claim to love. If following God and having a relationship with Jesus doesn't offer forgiveness when they mess up, I can promise you they will not want any part of that. They will never be able to develop an identity in Christ if they haven't felt what truly living in that identity can be.

### *Teach them that God has created them for a purpose and help them discover that purpose.*

In my twenty-nine-plus years of ministry, nowhere have I seen kids come to life more than when they serve others. I have been on mission's trips with outwardly selfish high school students and seen them melt when faced with the idea that they can be a conduit for God's love. I have seen middle school kids work harder than they thought they could work to provide for people in need. I have seen college students and young adults build relationships with people who look nothing like them and seek to love and serve those people wholeheartedly.

When kids, teens, and young adults step into living for a greater purpose than themselves, they come alive. This doesn't just have to happen on a mission's trip, it can happen every day. As parents, we have to help our kids discover what God is doing in them and how they can serve His purposes in the world. This is not easy as we fight the worldly tide that pushes them to live for themselves and "get yours." Teaching them to live for a higher purpose starts with the previous encouragement to help them embrace an identity that ties them to a higher power, Jesus. But, surrendering to God and seeking to live for Him doesn't automatically equal understanding your purpose in the world. I know many adults who are still trying to figure that out.

In order to help our kids discover their purpose (or at least start heading in a direction), we have to put them in situations where they can feel and experience what their purpose could be. I don't want to confuse this practice with trying on different identities. I simply believe we have to help our kids discover their identity and purpose

71

by helping them to experience what it might be. How can a kid know if part of their specific purpose is to serve the poor if they have never experienced what that feels like? How can our kids discover they have the gift of teaching if we don't put them in situations to use and develop that gift? We're good at working to help them improve their batting and grade point averages. What about their calling and purpose?

## Wrapping up the Identity Bag

Throughout this project, I have had a few people ask me, "Which one is the biggest bag?" I've tried hard not to rank them, but there is no doubt that the Identity Bag is toward the top of the list. It pained me to hear one college student say, "It's amazing how young people learn how to 'put a fake on'—this is bred into you from an early age." We're breeding a generation of kids who are learning how to be fake, and they have no idea who they really are. We do have an identity crisis!

In some ways, all of the bags pour into this one. The way we believe we have to perform shapes our identity. The way we learn how to deal with rejection impacts our identity. How we reconcile the guilt and shame we feel molds our identity. I could go on. If we as parents know about the identity baggage that our kids are potentially packing, we have to do something about it. I want my kids to be able to echo what I heard one college girl say in a focus group. "You are not defined by where you are involved, but by Jesus. I didn't understand the concept of having worth until I came to college."

I want my kids to feel like they have worth, and I don't want them to have to wait until college to feel it. I want them to know who they are in Christ and figure out how to live that out every day. I want them to know they are loved and have somewhere to truly belong and be themselves. I want them to have a purpose for their lives and discover how they can live out their purpose. I want them to feel comfortable in their identity and be free of the baggage that a lack of identity will inevitably lead them to pack.

## *Reflection Questions*

Take some time to reflect on your own sense of identity. What would you say defines you and where does your identity rest? How would your kids answer the question "I am _____"?

What are some ways you see your kids building their identity? Are they building a healthy foundation? Write down some ways you can actively help your kids build their identity in Christ.

Are your kids surrounded by adults and peers who help them build a solid identity? If so, how can you foster those relationships? If not, how can you help them develop the relationships they need to grow?

Does your family have a vision or mission statement? If so, what are some ways you are living it? If not, go to www.equipandencourage.com to download a resource to help you build one.

Is it difficult for you to offer grace and forgiveness to your kids (in a way they *feel* it)? If so, why and how can you change your mindset when it comes to this?

What are some things you can do to help your kids discover the purpose God has created them for?

**Endnotes**

[1] Kara Powell and Brad Griffin, *3 Big Questions That Change Every Teenager,* Baker Books, 2021, 35.

[2] Geoff Banks and James Banks, *Hope Lies Ahead: An Encouragement for Prayers of Prodigals From a Family That's Been There,* Our Daily Bread Publishing, 2020.

[3] Ibid., 27.

## Chapter Five
# The Comparison Bag

*"Once the first comparison is made, it's so easy to find yourself comparing yourself everywhere."—young adult*

This comment from a young adult in one of my focus groups said it all. He shared it in the context of how he grew up and how he frequently heard his parents making the comparison between him and his siblings. He was the youngest and remembered thinking that he wasn't good enough or capable of success because he was always looking at what others in his family were doing.

In the middle of working on this project, I went to lunch with a friend. He had asked me to spend some time with him to talk about some issues he was having with his elementary school-aged son. As the conversation moved along, I heard him say some things that linked to some baggage my friend had accumulated as a child. I decided to wade into those waters and ask him a few questions about his life and see where some of his thoughts were coming from. As soon as I mentioned the concept of "packing bags" it resonated with him. In his mind, my friend quickly moved away from the present and went right to the past. He stopped talking about his son and he started talking about his childhood and the struggles he had with his parents.

He talked about how his parents had spent years comparing him and his sister. He was more athletic and struggled in school, and he remembers his parents asking him, "Why can't you be more like your sister?" He remembered his parents asking his sister, "Why can't you be more athletic like your brother?" This friend was in his mid-thirties and there was no doubt these bags had lingered for years and years. I assume most parents aren't that blatant about it but, if we're not careful, we can subtly contribute to a culture of comparison that could live with our kids for a lifetime.

The next bag kids are packing today is the Comparison Bag. From an early age, we start walking around every day evaluating if we have what they have, if we get what they get, or if we look like they look. We ask questions like, "Am I as good as she is?" or "Am I getting as much as him?" I think it's human nature, and I think it started at the beginning of time. Not only do we compare ourselves to others, but we compare our lives to what we think we *could* (or worse yet, *should*) have. If we eat from that tree over there, we might just be able to have more wisdom, so let's do that (Genesis 3).

It's important to know this is yet another bag that gets packed in multiple ways and we, as parents, aren't solely responsible for the damage that can be done. As mentioned before, we are naturally wired to compare, and we often do it to ourselves. As we move through life, we also frequently get compared to others by our peers, teachers, coaches, and leaders.

But, if we're honest we have to admit, as parents, we *do* compare our kids. We just do, and it starts at an early age. If we have more than one kid, as soon as we start reaching milestones with our second child, the comparison is on:

- He's sleeping more or less than she did.
- She walked at nine months, and he didn't start until 11 months.
- He eats his vegetables, but she won't.
- She's better at math than he is.
- He's faster than his brother.

The list goes on. Our comparisons usually don't come from a critical place, and early on our kids are too young to understand what we are doing. But we do it. Often, when they begin to get a little older, we may stop verbally comparing them in front of each other, but they can feel it!

## Starts With Siblings

It happens almost every time. I'll have a project that needs to be done around the house and I'll enlist the help of my two kids. After we navigate the "why do we have to do this" conversation, the evaluation starts. I ask my son to start one part of the project and my daughter to start another. With one eye on the task at hand and the other eye on their sibling, you can see the wheels start turning in their minds. Then, the questions start.

"How come he's not helping me?"

"Why doesn't she have to do as much as I do?"

Or maybe we're getting ready for dinner and it's time to figure out whose turn it is to set and clear the table and who will wash the dishes. Depending on what kind of mood either of them is in, someone doesn't want to do their task for the night. We'll hear things like, "I did that last night!" or "It's her turn to do that."

Let's go a little deeper. What happens when it's time for my son and me to go on an annual father-son trip and my daughter wants to go too? She fails to remember all of the things we have done together over the past year and the fact that the two of us have a trip scheduled in a few months. All she sees is that he gets a fun trip and time with dad, and she doesn't.

My brother and his wife have three kids. They are all adults now, and they are very successful. My brother and his wife were (and are) great parents and are now amazing grandparents. As their kids went through their teen years, there were some choppy relational waters. Jason is the oldest and was a great athlete. He played quarterback at the local high school and did quite well. Our family had a history of playing QB at the school, with both me and my brother having played years earlier. The local newspaper did a great article on Jason and the family legacy. Being proud parents, Greg and Christine framed the article and put it on a wall in the upstairs hallway.

Jordan, two years younger, was not into sports at all. He is an amazing singer and performed all through high school in many ways. A few years later, a similar article was written about Jordan and his talents and, as parents would, they framed the article and posted it on the upstairs wall next to the article about Jason. Jason and Jordan both went to a great university located just a few hours away.

Caitlin is two years younger than Jordan. Caitlin played soccer, was involved in several school clubs, served in student government, and was an all-around great student. In her senior year, she applied to go to a local state university, one that Jason and Jordan did not get into. When she got her acceptance letter online, she printed it out, grabbed a marker, and walked upstairs to the family wall of fame. She taped her college acceptance letter next to the articles about Jason and Jordan and on it she wrote, "I win!"

I know that my brother and his wife were in no way trying to pack a comparison bag between their kids. I also know that it's never a bad idea to recognize and praise a child's success. What parent doesn't want to celebrate their kids' accomplishments? I just wonder how often I have done something similar and unknowingly planted a seed of sibling comparison baggage into my kids.

## With Friends and Peers

I remember watching the situation unfold for several years. Two high school guys were the best of friends and loved spending time with each other. They were both good-looking, athletic, intelligent, and all-around good kids. They played the same sports and enjoyed the same hobbies. They ran in the same crowd and both came to youth group at our church. They were both generally headed in the same direction in life and secretly both wanted to outdo the other.

On the surface, it looked like they were on the same page. Underneath, there was a spirit of competition and comparison that was always running in the background. One would succeed in a particular area and you could see the other offer a half-hearted congratulations. What made it worse was that one of their moms seemed to fan the flame of comparison. She was always boasting and bragging about how well her son was doing, even during the times when everyone else knew he wasn't. I began to wonder if the comparison trap her son was in had been rooted in his mom's need to tout her son as the best.

On some level, we all compare ourselves with our friends and peers. It's somewhat natural, but it also takes a toll on our souls. When we compare, we either win or we lose, and neither leads us to a good place. Our posture can either be one of superiority or despair, and we often don't know how to deal with either. Our kids certainly don't have the tools to navigate the emotions that come with being on one side or the other of the comparison game. They compare themselves to their friends and peers in school, sports, the arts, their looks, and their family finances. Kids whose families can afford them compare their cars, their vacations, and their experiences. Adolescents have always compared their toys, but it seems like the toys and opportunities just keep getting bigger and bigger.

There is no doubt that technology has put our kids in a different world when it comes to comparing themselves to their friends and peers. Smart phones and social media make comparing a part of everyday life for most kids. Before they even get to the apps and content, they compare the devices themselves. If you have model 8 of a device and your friend gets model 10, well that stinks for you. We addressed a big part of this in the Performance Bag when talking about performance with peers and the "new lunchroom." If you haven't read that part yet, I would encourage you to take a moment to look at it.

## *With the World*

"Back in the day" (when we parents were growing up), our comparisons often stopped with what we could learn about people in our general area. I remember having to wait for the Saturday newspaper to compare myself and my Friday night performance with other local athletes who played my sport and position. Again, thanks to the world wide web and social media, we can compare ourselves to someone across the globe almost instantly. I remember being a young youth pastor talking about how we shouldn't be comparing ourselves to what we see in magazines or tabloids (boy has that changed). For kids today, the comparison with what is happening in the world is non-stop.

I know of middle and high school athletes who have created social media accounts where they share their stats and highlights with whoever will follow. Teens who follow these accounts compare their performance and work hard to shine brighter on the court or field. The people they are competing with aren't friends or peers, just someone "out there" who has set some sort of bar to cross. As kids (and parents) learn about trends such as starting college early and graduating high school with tons of college credit, the comparison game is on and the potential baggage starts to build. Teens think, "If I don't get on that path then I'll fall behind and be less likely to succeed in the future." Much of this Comparison Baggage is nudging some kids into increased apathy. If I can't be as good as others, what's the point? I'll just give up.

The ever-present issue of body image (especially for girls) can pack some tremendous baggage that is incredibly hard to overcome. Gone are the days when young girls had to buy a magazine or see a movie to compare themselves to a star or super model. Now they just have to scroll on their phone for a few moments to see images they will likely never be able to live up to. In talking about this issue, one young lady said, "It plays out in how I see myself, how I think men see me, and how I see other women as well. It's heavy and it's something I can't run away from."

## The Burden of the Bag:
## What Happens if the Comparison Bag Gets Packed?

It seems as if comparison baggage is being packed all the time. If we carry it, we are all impacted in different ways. I do think some common things happen to our kids if they pack comparison bags. They could:

- Always feel inadequate—When kids and teens are constantly reminded they don't measure up to others, they begin to feel like they are simply not enough.

- Feel superior and act as if they are better than everyone else—On the other hand, if kids and teens are somewhat successful in the world, they can begin to read their own headlines, believe they are somehow better than the people around them, and treat those people poorly.

- Live in a constant state of stress and anxiety—There is no doubt that the comparison culture we live in contributes to the stress and anxiety our kids feel. When you are constantly measuring where you stand in the world, you expend a tremendous amount of emotional energy.

- Create relational distance with family members—If kids feel like they are being compared to others in their family (usually in a bad way), they may intentionally or subconsciously want to get away from those people. No one wants to be in a community where they feel like they are at the bottom of the list.

- Develop a personality of judgment and jealousy—When you constantly compare what you have and who you are to others in the world, you can naturally become judgmental and jealous. Your heart toward others can grow cold, and you can find yourself pulling against them.

82

# Lightening the Load:
# Fighting the Comparison Bag

### *Don't set up a culture of comparison in your home.*

Boy, this is hard! It's sometimes easy to use comparison as a tool to attempt to motivate our children. "See what he's doing? Why don't you just do that!" As tempting as this motivational strategy is, it ultimately doesn't work and may plant long-term seeds of resentment. As the key culture setters in our home, we as parents have to make sure we don't set up a culture of comparison, but rather a culture of celebration (more on that to come). Because it is a natural human tendency to compare (and my kids are doing it anyway), I need to work extra hard not to let my kids think I am weighing one of them against the other.

Not only do I need to make sure I'm not comparing my kids to one another, but I also need to refrain from comparing my kids to their friends and peers. If I tell one of my kids that I expect them to behave or perform more like one of their friends, they may wonder if I would rather that kid be my son or daughter. They may become frustrated with that friend and distance themselves from that relationship. I need to remember and teach my kids that we have all sinned and fallen short of the glory of God (Romans 3:23) and there are no perfect people. I need to decide that my home will not be a place where we play the comparison game.

### *Don't play the comparison game yourself.*

As mentioned before, it's true that "more is caught than taught." Having lived in the adult world for almost thirty years, I can attest to the fact that most of us play some version of the comparison game. We compare ourselves with our peers, with what they have accomplished and what toys they have. We compare ourselves at work and we wonder where we stand with the boss or powers that be. We compare ourselves to where we think we should be in life, and we are almost always disappointed. Because we play this game so much, it seeps out onto our kids. They catch it, and they start to play the same game at an early age. They see us comparing ourselves to others, and they think that's just the way of the world.

Learning how not to play the comparison game is a discipline. It starts with gratitude and contentment. In Philippians 4:11b-13, the apostle Paul says, "I have learned to be content whatever the circumstances. I know what it is to be in need, and I know what it is to have plenty. I have learned the secret of being content in any and every situation, whether well fed or hungry, whether living in plenty or in want. I can do all this through him [Christ] who gives me strength." Note that Paul says he has learned how to do these things, and it is Christ who gives him the strength to do it. If we are going to help our kids not compare themselves to so many people and situations, we have to learn how to do it first.

### *Encourage them to be their best, not the best (Heard this before?).*

Did I mention that the bags overlap? The things we can do to fight against them do too. Steering away from encouraging our kids to be *the* best can go against everything we have learned as adults and so many things they are learning as kids. They hear it all the time: "You have to be the best!" I'm all about encouraging kids to work hard and reach for the stars. But you know on every team, in every class, in every company, in every field, there's only *one* best. When kids are younger and they're not *the best*, they typically know it. For some kids, it motivates them to work harder but, for most kids, the comparison game they play eats at their identity every day.

What if we always encouraged them to do *their* best and celebrated that? There will no doubt be times (probably many of them) where their best doesn't necessarily propel them to the winner's circle. It's possible that their best (in some areas) may not be very good at all. Don't worry, I'm not a "trophy for every kid" guy, but I am a "help kids grow up healthy" guy. When kids live in a world where they are always pushed to be *the best* and they most often can't live up to those expectations, they tend to crash and burn at some point.

Learn to celebrate their effort. If they truly are working as hard as they can at something, let them know how proud you are of them for that. When you see them develop the discipline they will need so often in the future, help them understand that learning how to go through the process is incredibly valuable and will serve them well. As you see progress in any area, encourage them to take another step along the journey toward their desired destination.

### Teach them they are uniquely created by God to be themselves (not who you want them to be).

Indeed, our kids often don't know who they are and what they want to do in life. The age-old question, "What do you want to be when you grow up?" starts hitting them at an early age, and they begin to equate what they are going to do in life (their vocation) with who God has created them to be. We've already talked about some of this in earlier chapters, and there is more to come.

What if instead of letting them look around at what others are doing (comparison), we helped them discover what God has planted in them? Let's be honest, we all have hopes and dreams about the path we want our kids to take, but there's a big problem with that. It's our path, not theirs. As kids grow up, let them pursue the things they want to pursue and don't compare their life and preferred experiences with yours or anyone else's. This is hard. I hope for my kids to have some of the same experiences I did and have some of the same interests my wife and I have. I think it's okay for us to have dreams like these for our children, but things can take an ugly turn when these dreams are interpreted as expectations.

If you have multiple kids, you have to remember that every child is different and, not only has God wired our offspring differently from us, He has wired them different from each other. We need to lead each child to find his or her God-given talents, gifts, and passions, and we need to help them step into their identity without the fear of not measuring up to something or someone.

### *Teach them to pursue humility, which combats pride.*

Some kids end up on the *good* side of the comparison game. They seem to always get it right, always win the game, or always be in the right place at the right time. This can lead to confidence that can easily creep into arrogance. If we can teach our kids how to be humble and understand that every gift they have comes from God, they will be less likely to develop an unhealthy pride that fuels comparison.

Humility does not come easily and is not natural, especially in a world and culture that teaches us all to share and tout our accomplishments. If your kids have social media, make sure you are watching what they post. If you see them bragging on themselves, have a conversation about what it means to develop and display real humility.

Finally, make sure you are modeling the humility you are hoping your kids will display. We've all met (and been) the parent that talks about, shares, and posts about the family accomplishments. This is tricky because we all want to celebrate our kids and our families when good things come our way. I know I do. If we want our kids to learn humility, we have to work hard to make sure the example they see exhibits the behavior we are hoping they will display.

*Help them discover their strengths and gifts and give them pathways to express those.*

As our kids are growing up, they often struggle with knowing how they are skilled and gifted. They try many activities when they are younger, but they usually focus on a few things in late elementary and early middle school. They may try something for a while because a friend is trying it, or they feel like we want them to try it. The truth is they may not even like it. So many kids find themselves years down the road in a sport or activity only to finally admit they no longer want to stay on that particular path. They often feel as if they are trapped and can't move on to a new interest because they may disappoint the adults in their life. They know how much time and money we have invested in their experiences, and they are not sure they have the freedom to walk away.

One of our main jobs is to fan the flames of interest our kids display, at all phases. We have to remember they are growing and changing in so many ways, and their interests are growing and changing too. That little boy who loved practicing and playing soccer may quickly morph into a young man who wants to learn guitar and join a band. That little girl who loved dolls and Legos may move toward making videos and starting a YouTube channel. Obviously, we need to make sure our kids' interests are appropriate and safe. At the same time, we need to help them explore their changing interests and land in a place where they are fulfilled.

I feel like I need to finish this section with this statement: Don't forget that it's their life, not ours. We all know the temptation to steer our kids into what we like and what we think they should do. After all, they are still developing and learning how to think—what do they know? There is a real tension here, as we often do know what's best for our kids, but only to an extent. In a world with so many choices and pathways, our job as parents is to help our kids find the one that is right for them, that best fits their gifts, and the one God has set before them. Even though their life is theirs to live, we need to constantly remind them that God has given them their life and He has a plan for them.

### *Teach them to celebrate the success of others.*

One of the things we can do starting at a very early age is to help our kids learn how to celebrate the success of others. It's easy and natural to celebrate when you do well. What about when someone else excels? What if we teach our kids to authentically celebrate when their siblings accomplish things instead of being jealous? What if we model celebrating when our friends accomplish things to let our kids know that all of life is not a competition? When we can celebrate the accomplishments of others, we don't worry so much about our own accomplishments. It's all about taking the focus off of "me" and understanding that life is about encouraging and serving others.

## Wrapping up the Comparison Bag

One of the ironies of writing this chapter (and this whole book) is the comparison issue I am currently dealing with in my own life. Even though I consider myself a pretty stable person, I have a ton of experience in ministry, and I have a fair amount of ministry "success" (whatever that means), I still find myself playing the comparison game. I don't think I have a ton of comparison baggage from my childhood, but the pattern of comparing myself to others certainly has some root. I look around at other leaders in ministry and I compare my platform, my voice, and my ministry to theirs. I almost always feel like I am "losing," and it makes me frustrated and judgmental. I don't like the person I become when my mind goes down that road. I've learned that this pattern is hard to overcome, which is why I don't want my kids to pack any comparison baggage or develop any comparison patterns.

Comparison feeds insecurity. Comparison breeds jealousy. Playing the comparison game can create a life of instability and can lead us to never look up or look forward because we are always looking around. When we pack comparison baggage, it can not only stay with us for a long time, but it can also push us into a never-ending cycle of comparison. The bag keeps getting bigger. Unlike some of the other bags that only get packed in certain situations, the struggle of comparison can come at any time. We compare in our homes, we compare at work, we compare on social media, and we compare with our friends. If we don't pay attention, comparison just becomes a part of how we operate.

I see Steve every now and again. We went to high school together and were pretty good friends. Steve was a good athlete, a good student, and an overall popular kid. As I reflect on those teenage years, there is no doubt in my mind that Steve played the comparison game pretty hard with a lot of people. He was a part of our friend group, but he lived "on the other side of the tracks" if you know what I mean. His family struggled financially and was in a bit of a different situation than the rest of the crew. You could see him always trying to keep up and often trying to *one-up* people around him. I can't say for sure, but I think he packed some rather big comparison baggage during those years.

I see this baggage come out in the way he talks about the past, his attitude toward others, and his overall personality. I think he's hurting inside for a lot of reasons, and I think comparison has a lot to do with that. I wonder how Steve would be different today if he had not developed a pattern of comparison and not seemingly packed so much comparison baggage. He and his wife have divorced, and I feel like I see him playing another version of the comparison game (that many of us play) as he tries to elevate his kids and their accomplishments on social media. I also know that, although he is a friend and I like him, I don't want my kids ending up like Steve because they never learned how to deal with comparing themselves to others and the burden that creates.

As parents, we are uniquely positioned to lead our kids away from living a life of comparison. We can help them guard their hearts and minds and know they are enough for us, and for God. They don't need to measure up to anyone or anything else, and we need to help them feel that. If we can help them walk away from developing a comparison mindset, they will no doubt be able to see and celebrate their own successes as well as have a better chance at building a solid foundation for the rest of life.

## *Reflection Questions*

As you were growing up, did you ever feel the pressure of comparison? If so, how did the "comparison game" impact you?

If you have more than one child, how are they the same and how are they different? How can you celebrate them individually despite their differences?

Do you ever find yourself comparing your kids in front of them? How might this practice be impacting them in a negative way?

Do you see your kids comparing themselves to others around them or people in the world? How do you think their tendency to compare is playing into their emotional health?

What are some things you can do to help your kids embrace and exercise humility in their life?

Do you see social media having a negative impact on your children's attitude? What are some ways you can help them navigate this?

What are some ways you can help your kids discover and exercise their unique gifts and talents?

## Chapter Six
# The Authority Bag

*"It's hard to respect authority, especially when adults make decisions you don't like. I often voice my disagreement when I shouldn't."—college student*

I was talking to a friend recently and he shared about how he was struggling with leading a few young adults who work for him. His organization had made a particular decision that would impact his staff and their responsibilities. In a meeting one day, he communicated this decision to the team and they quickly met him with, "We can't do that!" He was a bit dismayed. He continued to push and explained why this decision was best. They continued to push and told him that the "request" was not possible, and they simply could not do it. As we talked about the situation and the relational dynamics that were at play, we both identified something. He was dealing with an authority issue. First off, these young adults, who were being paid for their services, looked at the conversation as a request more than a directive by their boss. Secondly, they felt perfectly comfortable saying "no" to the authority figure who was leading them. He's a great leader who has produced some great results over the years. He loves his team and leads them with real intentionality. He also is leading a group of people who, in my opinion, have packed some real *Authority Baggage* over the years that is coming out as they live their lives.

93

I don't know about you, but life in my family can sometimes feel like a non-stop power struggle. Thankfully, the fight is rarely between my wife and me, but it is often between our kids and us. Almost every day we battle with getting our kids to obey and do what we ask when we ask it. They push the boundaries of authority and, especially in their teenage years, they want us to give them the control of their lives they think they deserve. When we use the authority over our children that we have been given by God, they often don't know how to emotionally handle it. That may be a poor reflection on the two of us as parents, but I suspect it's where many of you live as well.

Kids today struggle with obeying authority and, because of this, they are packing some serious baggage that will impact them for years. As they grow up, adolescents (and adults) are asking a few questions when it comes to authority:

- Who's in charge of me, really?
- Do I have ultimate power and control over my life?
- If I (as the child) don't yet have full control of my life, when will I get there?

These are questions I remember struggling with as I grew up. I see my teenage kids asking them now. I knew my parents were in charge and I had to follow their lead, but it was hard. From probably late elementary school to early college, we danced a dance where I gained more and more control and eventually gained the freedom that all teenagers and young adults seek. I don't know if this is new, but it does seem like kids today increasingly think they are in charge of their lives at an earlier and earlier age and they don't have to follow any real authority. Just watch many families operate and you can see the kids running the show, even if parents think they are.

While there is no question that children are a gift from God, it sometimes seems like we have elevated them to be the center of the family. Whether deliberately or inadvertently, it can often feel like all things revolve around them. In our quest to give our kids the best lives possible, their schedules begin to dictate our lives. We want to give them all the opportunities we had (or wish we had had). Often, family decisions are made by starting with the kids and their activities. This can, at times, send a subliminal message to kids that they are the center of the universe. Have you ever been in a situation where you had a commitment, or maybe there was a family commitment, and your child was going to have to miss an activity or a game? To them, it felt like the end of the world. My wife and I have been in that situation a handful of times, and it's led us to reevaluate what is most important. We've had to sit down with our kids and explain that, while their activities have importance, as parents and adults we have things we need to take care of too. We need to help them understand that some things will have to take precedence over what they are involved in.

There are times when we, as parents, can subtly contribute to authority baggage in other ways. A few years ago, our son was on a basketball team in a local rec league. The coach of the team was *awful*! The guy acted like he knew what he was doing, but he had no clue. The players were constantly frustrated, and the parents were struggling with his coaching style. After one game where the coach had made some crazy decisions, I had to work hard to hold my tongue. When we got in the car to go home, everything in me wanted to talk about how bad the coach was. I wanted to say, "Could you believe when he did that? How stupid!" It actually could have been a bonding moment for me and my son. "What was he thinking?" seemed like an appropriate question to discuss with my teenage son.

I was right in the middle of writing this book and I realized that, if I led my son into a conversation about how bad this guy was, I would probably be planting a seed that talking poorly about an authority figure is okay. I would have modeled what it looks like to question and criticize authority. I would have contributed to some potential Authority Baggage that would be difficult to unpack. Are there times when we need to question authority, step in, and protect our kids? Absolutely. Do we do that more often than we should? Probably.

Our kids need to learn to trust, respect, and follow authority. This is not because we want to be rulers in our homes and build little robots who will obey our every demand (at least it shouldn't be). They need to follow authority because God has set up the world that way. That is His plan and His system, especially in the context of family. Now, I wouldn't lead with that logic with your kids, especially if they are still sorting out what they believe about God. But, as we have and will talk about, I would model it. If our kids don't learn to believe in and follow authority in their lives, the consequences will be real, painful, and long-term. If they can't learn to trust and follow the authority of teachers and coaches, how will they learn to trust and follow a boss? If they don't believe that rules and laws are in place for a reason, they will break these rules and laws and suffer the consequences. Opportunities will be lost, relationships will be broken, and they will likely live a very lonely life as they continue to put themselves at the center of their world.

## *Entitlement*

Have you ever been around someone who acts as if they deserve something? I have. It seems like more and more these days I am around people who want to essentially get something for nothing.

The thought of having to put your head down and work, and work hard, is becoming a lost art. I know of college students and young adults who start jobs and believe they immediately have the right to speak into the way things are being done. They overestimate the importance of their role and they overvalue their potential contribution. That sounds harsh, but so many people do not understand the chain of command and they don't respect authority. They believe they should get what they want, have a voice, and have a greater amount of control (and have it soon). They seem to think it's a right. I wonder where they get it from.

Unfortunately, our desire for our kids to have the best life possible can easily lead them to develop a sense of entitlement. It seems like many parents are quick to jump to the defense of their kids. We are more likely to get involved to solve their problems. One way we see this is in how parents interact with coaches and teachers. About a decade ago, a political cartoon came out that demonstrated how things have changed over the years. The cartoon depicted a set of parents holding a child's report card that showed a list of bad grades. One side of the cartoon had the parents and the teacher together demanding an answer from their child as to why the grades were bad. The year was 1969. The other side of the cartoon had the parents and their child together demanding an answer from the teacher as to why the grades were bad. The year was 2009. Regrettably, this mindset seems to be a growing trend and undermines the authority of the teacher.

We see entitlement creeping into this generation in other ways as well. Kids are being hard-wired for instant gratification through technology, devices, games, and social media. When my wife and I were young, we would watch maybe an hour or two of TV a day. To be honest, that was about all the programming TV had for our age. The rest of the programming didn't interest us. Now, there are channels and streaming services designated with non-stop programming for almost every stage of childhood. Whereas cartoons used to be a treat you could only watch on Saturday mornings, now you can have them on demand. My wife says when the kids were young, she was quite thankful for this when she needed an hour in the middle of the day to get something done or just take a short break. Now she feels like she often has to wage war with the kids to get them interested in doing something that is not on a screen. This is a battle our parents did not have to fight, partly because there was hardly anything on TV we wanted to watch. I don't think many of us were interested in "As the World Turns." The point is that this generation of kids is used to having and receiving so many things they want when they want it, rarely having to wait at all.

Remember before cell phones when we would have to wait at home for someone to return our call? Now, in the age of text and other messaging, even we as adults often expect an immediate response when we reach out to someone. I find myself checking messages mere moments after I have sent something to see if the small bubbles appear indicating a response is coming soon. And therein lies the problem. Instead of being hopeful or thankful or patient for something, it becomes an expectation or a demand.

Sometimes as parents we also play into their entitlement mentality. When we help things come more easily for our kids, they can begin to expect that things should be easy. When our daughter's iPad stopped working, she simply expected that we would get her a new one. There was no ask. No, "Can you please fix this one or get me a new one?" There was just an expectation that this device is a part of life and we, as her parents, had an obligation to provide her a new one. Whether it is quickly replacing something for them that got lost or broken or stepping in to "help" solve a problem with a teacher or even friends, our children don't learn to work hard to take care of their belongings or sort through difficulties. Again, this leads to entitlement.

### *What does entitlement have to do with authority?*

Entitlement can quickly breed a lack of respect for authority. When kids become entitled, they become selfish. As we've mentioned, they begin to think they deserve things instead of being appreciative of all the good they have in life. Life becomes all about me. "*I* deserve this." "*I* shouldn't have to work for that." "Those rules don't apply to *me*." "Why should someone else have the right to tell *me* how to live or what to do?" "Who are you to tell *me* what to do?" What becomes dangerous about this mentality is that not only do they begin to lose respect for human authority in their life, it also erodes their respect for God's authority in their life.

Our pastor often says, "If God created life, then He gets to define it." God is the ultimate authority. He has the right to tell us what is right and what is wrong. Fortunately for us, God is good, and He has promised us "life… to the full" (John 10:10) as we seek to follow and obey Him. As followers of Christ, our call is to submit to His plan for our life. However, it is not easy to die to oneself or to put others first. This is difficult for even the most committed disciples. Can you imagine how much more difficult it becomes, and how foreign it sounds, to someone who has had all their wants and needs provided for on-demand and their problems are taken care of by others?

## *The Other Side of the Coin*

On one side of the coin, we see a generation growing up feeling entitled. Yet in talking with students, another theme arose—those who saw their parents as their authority, but *only* as that. In these students' eyes, their parents had authority without having a real relationship with them. One student said, "Parents have authority but not the relational equity to talk about real things."

The problem with this side of the coin is that parents miss out on really being able to invest in the lives of their kids. They may have their children's obedience and, to an extent, their respect, but they do not have nearly the amount of influence on their child's moral compass as they could. I remember a wise mentor first introducing me to the shift from control to influence. When our kids are young, we have a lot of control over what they do, where they go, and what they experience. As they grow from kids to teens to young adults, that control steadily goes away. It's inevitable. The goal is to have influence with them when they are older, and the only way we can have influence is to have a relationship. Because parents often focus on the control side of things and lose the influence, some students we interviewed said they were instead looking to people outside of their home to form their opinions and beliefs.

As I was talking to a fellow parent about this book, he brought up a great question: "What do you want your greatest investment to be?" Then he noted, "We're more interested in *providing for* our kids than *investing in them*." Or, in some cases, we may be more interested in their obedience than their development. We may struggle with control and need to get them to where we want them to be. One young adult told me, "I only see my parents as parents. I don't see them as someone I can talk to. I only see them as an authority, but I've never seen them as anything else. They have not proven that they are there to guide me, they just want to make decisions for me."

There is no question that God designed parents to have authority over children. He explicitly commands children to obey their parents. Children obeying their parents is a great representation and reminder for God's children to obey their heavenly Father. Being too permissive and allowing too much negotiation erodes a child's understanding of the importance of submitting to authority. However, we can swing too far on the other side of the pendulum as well. Ultimately, the goal of parenting is not an obedient child, but a child who desires to follow Christ and is using their spiritual gifts to serve Him. Yet, teaching obedience plays a large role in this. Paul Tripp, in his book *Parenting: 14 Gospel Principles That Can Radically Change Your Family*, puts it like this:

> Here's God's amazing plan. He makes his invisible authority visible by sending visible authority figures as his representatives. This means that every time you exercise authority in the lives of your children, it must be a beautiful picture of the authority of God. In the lives of your children, you are the look of God's face, you are the touch of his hand, and you are the tone of his voice. You must never exercise authority in an angry, impatient way. You must never exercise authority in an abusive way. You must never exercise authority in a selfish way. Why? Because you have been put into your position as parent to display before your children how beautiful, wise, patient, guiding, protective, rescuing, and forgiving God's authority is.[1]

When we approach discipline with this mindset, not only are we teaching our kids to submit to authority, we are also building relational equity, which allows us to have more influence in our kids' lives as they get older.

## The Burden of the Bag:
## What Happens if the Authority Bag Gets Packed?

If kids develop authority baggage, it can lead them into some real frustration and difficult situations in their adult lives. Depending on how much they struggle with authority, the consequences could be rather small, or they could be huge. Based on my observations and experience, if our kids pack the authority bag, they could:

- Become self-centered—Part of why we buck authority at times is because we want to be in ultimate control of our lives. It becomes all about what I think is best for me. This mentality can quickly lead to self-centeredness.

- Become entitled—When kids believe they deserve every-thing and they can work around the rules to get what they want, they can quickly become entitled. Instead of having a demeanor of gratitude, it becomes a demeanor of demand.

- Have a hard time trusting and following any authority in their life—If kids begin to believe the only person they have to answer to is themselves, it erodes the authority of anyone else in their lives.

- Struggle with God as an authority—If the authority of parents, teachers, and coaches has been undermined as kids grow up, they will have difficulty submitting to the authority of a boss and ultimately, even of God.

- Spend a lifetime dealing with difficult consequences—Eventually, the lack of respect for authority will catch up to kids as they become adults. The reality is when we do not submit to authority, whether man's or God's, consequences will come.

## Lightening the Load:
## Fighting the Authority Bag

### *Model being under and respecting authority.*

As hard as it may be for us as adults, we need to do everything we can to model being under authority ourselves. That means not talking bad about our boss when he or she makes a decision we disagree with. It means living under the authority of elected officials, even if you disagree with their policies. It means not criticizing our parents as they make decisions and try to influence us in our adult years. During a recent holiday break, I kind of dismissed a request my mom made of the entire family. My teenage daughter said, "Wow dad. Way to follow the wishes of your mom." Ouch! Although relationships have morphed and the context is different, we are still called by God to honor our father and mother. If we are a part of a local church, we should never badmouth or criticize the pastors and leaders God has put in place and we should seek to follow their lead. If we can't model being under authority ourselves, how can we expect our kids to do it?

Also, we should continue to live out our faith by being under the authority of God. There are certainly thoughts and decisions that we all need to bring to the Lord and submit to His authority. Talk with your kids about hard decisions you have made because you wanted to be obedient to God. Let your children in on how you have been obedient to the Lord and the benefits you received from doing so, even when it was difficult.

### *Give your kids opportunities to serve others.*

This may sound odd, but if part of the problem with respecting authority is entitlement and self-centeredness, then part of the solution is to learn to get outside of oneself and help meet the needs of others. Philippians 2:3, states, "Do nothing out of selfish ambition or vain conceit. Rather, in humility value others above yourselves." We experience putting others first by actually doing it. I have seen kids, teenagers, and young adults become transformed because their eyes have been opened to a bigger world than the one they live in every day. Hearts soften and seeds are planted. The idea of living for something bigger than yourself can be powerful.

By serving, we are ultimately submitting to God's authority. Change takes place in our hearts when we not only see the needs of others but see how God can use us to help meet those needs. We step into truly being the hands and feet of Christ in the world and we begin to believe that God can make a difference through us. With this softening of the heart, kids may be more open to submitting to God's authority in other areas of their lives as well.

### *Teach them to follow authority, not just yours.*
If they have a problem with a teacher or a coach, try your hardest *not* to intervene and fix the problem. Kids need to learn how to follow the authority they are under, even when they disagree or it's hard. Coach your children through respectfully talking with adults in authority to resolve the problem themselves. There are obviously times when our kids are not ready to handle things on their own and we as parents need to step in, but these times should be few and far between. The last thing we want is to raise kids who are incapable of navigating issues and problems when they become adults. Many kids today are being wired to walk away from conflict and issues because it's easier to move on. The only way to help them grow in this area is to let them exercise this muscle as they grow up.

*Follow through in your discipline and don't negotiate.*

Kids need to know that we mean what we say. One of the worst things we as parents can do to undermine our authority is to back down on what we say or allow our kids and teens to negotiate their way out of a consequence. This means we need to think about what we are going to say before we say it. We need to take the time to determine what an appropriate disciplinary action might be before we proclaim it to be. How many times have you, in your anger and frustration, taken something away from your kids or given them a punishment that didn't fit the crime? I know I have. At times it may be appropriate to acknowledge that we overreacted and issued too harsh of a punishment, but for the most part we need to learn to discipline ourselves to stay calm, think, appropriately discipline, and stand our ground no matter how hard it is on us. If our toddler or preschooler throws a fit because they can't have the candy they want, we have to be willing to endure that fit and help them understand the answer is "no." If we take away our ten-year-old's device for a few days, we have to be willing to engage them in a different way instead of pushing them away and punishing them relationally too. If our teenager drives and we take away the car because they miss curfew, we have to be willing to drive them to school and work.

I have a friend that introduced me to a phrase a few years ago. He encouraged me, in my discipline with my kids, to say, "Obey without delay." My kids needed to learn to obey immediately, no matter what. My kids have grown to hate this phrase, but it has helped them to be a little faster in their replies. I feel like I hear, "Yes sir" a lot quicker than I used to. They don't always follow through in what they say "yes" to, but that's another issue and at least we're making progress.

*Explain the reasons for your family rules and expectations.*

Do you remember how much you hated it when your parents told you the reason you had to do something was "because I said so"? It was maddening. If I'm honest, I have caught myself saying that same thing to my children in the heat of the moment as well and I see how much it infuriates my kids. One young adult said it this way, "Nothing carries less weight than 'Because I said so.'"

To begin with, we need to make sure we have the right reasons for asking for obedience. In addition to having our family run smoothly, our rules should also help develop godly character in our children. If that is the purpose of the rule or request, we should clue our kids into it. Often, if children understand (even if they don't agree with) the reason behind the request, they are more likely to obey it. As I develop in my leadership skills, I have learned that people are more likely to get behind the *what* when they understand the *why*. The same is true of our kids.

### *Teach them the purpose of God's ultimate authority.*

As our Creator, God has ultimate authority over us. He knows what is best for us whether we believe it or not. Scripture tells us over and over again how much He loves us and desires for us to prosper. In Josh McDowell's book *Right From Wrong,* he explains that all of God's rules have one of two purposes—either to provide for us or to protect us. When our kids truly understand God's heart for them, His desire to protect them from harm and negative consequences, and to provide them with abundant life, it may make it easier for them to submit to His authority.

### *Encourage them to follow Jesus.*

Most of us would agree it is easier to obey God when we believe and trust that He really loves us and wants what is best for us. This starts with having a real relationship with God through Jesus. You are the primary spiritual influence in your child's life. Do what you can to help them develop a sincere relationship with Jesus that will help them learn to submit. Real power and change will occur in your children's lives when they are walking with Jesus and allowing the Holy Spirit to move in them. If they just try to submit to and follow authority apart from a relationship with God, they will simply be building a system of rules to follow.

### *Pray for their hearts.*

Unfortunately, rebellion against authority is a consequence we all experience as a result of our sin. We should not be surprised when we see this play out in our kids' relationship with us. One of the most effective and powerful things we can do for our kids is to pray for them. And one of the most effective and powerful ways to pray for them is by praying Scripture over them. One, in particular, that may help with keeping this bag from being packed is Psalm 25:4-5. Instead of praying it for yourself, replace the "me" in the Scripture with your child's name:

"Show _____ your ways, Lord, teach _____ your paths; guide _____ in your truth and teach _____, for you are God _____'s Savior, and _____'s hope is in you all day long."

## Wrapping up the Authority Bag

Over the years I've heard many adults talk about the struggle with authority. We've all been there. I hope I've made progress in that area of life but, if I'm honest, that baggage surfaces often. I can easily fall into thinking, "It's not my fault" or "I don't need them" and I hear my kids doing the same. A culture of blame (fueled by the entitlement we've already discussed) creates an environment that struggles to submit to anyone for anything.

This chapter feels a little heavier to me than others. I think it is because if we are not careful as parents, we can contribute a lot to our kids packing this particular bag in several ways, and I believe the concept of authority goes right to the heart of our ability to trust and follow God (more on that in a moment). I've heard stories of parents calling *college* coaches to berate them because they are not happy with their son or daughter's playing time. I've heard of parents joining young adults in job interviews because they are not happy with the benefits that are being offered. I know of people who openly criticize and question the pastors and spiritual authorities that God has put in their life. The truth is that the inability to model following authority can so easily leak out onto our kids if we aren't careful.

In some ways, authority is directly linked to trust. As a follower of Christ, I need to trust Him in every way. That trust should lead me to place Jesus at the center of my life and give all authority to Him. If I, as an adult and as a parent, can actually do that and model what it looks like, my kids will see a picture of what it looks like to follow authority. If I place my trust in God to provide for me and my family, to comfort me in times of need, and to lead me to the abundant life I crave, then my kids will have a front-row seat to watch what a real life of faith looks like. Then, when I encourage them to develop a real trust for me and for God, they have a picture of what that could be. When we ask them to follow our authority (that comes from and flows from God), they may be more likely to do it.

When it comes to disciplining our kids, parents can often go in one of two directions. We can either come across too hard and breed resentment and relational distance, or we can work to be our kids' "buddies" and exercise little authority at all. Neither extremes are good and both can add to the Authority Bag. It's a fine line to walk. I hope I haven't left you feeling like you are in a no-win situation—if you are too permissive you screw your kids up, but if you're too authoritarian you'll never have a relationship with them.

How can I make sure I have just the right balance? I don't want to contribute to the lie that we can be perfect parents if we could just figure everything out. So, I want to remind you God is sovereign, and our mistakes cannot thwart His plan. He uses everything for good, even our shortcomings. The health and success of our kids do not lay solely on our shoulders. He is a God of grace, and His grace covers us, including our parenting. He is our authority and James 4:7 tells us to "submit yourselves to God." It all starts there.

Our kids are then told in the Ten Commandments and reminded in Ephesians 6:1-3: "Children, obey your parents in the Lord, for this is right. 'Honor your father and mother'—which is the first commandment with a promise—'so that it may go well with you and that you may enjoy long life on the earth.'"

I hope and pray it will go well with my children and they will enjoy an abundant, long life on the earth and an eternal life with God. Ironically, I want them to enjoy freedom in life that only comes from understanding and following authority.

## *Reflection Questions*

What is your view of authority and following the leaders in your life? How might your views of authority be impacting your kids' views of authority?

Are there things you do or say that subtly erode your kids' view of authority in the world? How can you discipline yourself to refrain from criticizing authority in front of your kids?

Do you see your kids struggling to follow authority? If so, how can you help them grow in this area? If not, how can you help them continue with this mindset?

Do you or your kids seem to exhibit a sense of entitlement in life? What are some things you can do to change this mindset and help your family live more humbly?

Do you find yourself giving in to your kids when they push back on your discipline? Are their times when you find yourself disciplining your kids for things they do that aren't wrong or sinful, they just bug you? How can you ensure you have the right reasons for imposing discipline?

Are you taking the time to explain the "why" behind the things you are asking your kids to do? How can you help your kids better understand the importance of God's authority in their lives?

Take some time to pray for the hearts of your kids. Reflect on Psalm 25:4-5.

**Endnotes**

[1] Paul Tripp, *Parenting: 14 Gospel Principles That Can Radically Change Your Family*, Crossway, 2016, 116.

## Chapter Seven

# The Rejection Bag

*"It amazes me that the most included people can still feel left out. You can be accepted by everyone else but get rejected by one person and that trumps all."—college student*

As I sat at the top of the bleachers and watched the game, my eyes and attention kept gravitating left. My middle school daughter and I were attending a high school football game (she loves football—dad win!) and we were just behind the student section. You know the area. It's the space where a large tribe of 9–12 graders somehow think they are on an island of their own and no adult is paying attention. Aside from hearing multiple "F-bombs" and trying not to watch a couple basically make out with each other for over an hour, I saw multiple teenagers struggle to fit in and find their place.

One young man (he looked like he was a ninth grader) particularly caught my attention. When he arrived, he didn't seem to see anyone he knew. I was impressed that this seemingly new freshman had come to the game by himself hoping to find some friends. He walked up the bleachers to one of the top rows where there was some space to stand behind the mob. As is normally the case with teens, there were a lot of little clusters of friends who were not really watching the game, but just enjoying the social scene. This young man spent the better part of an hour looking for someone to talk to and somewhere to belong. He tried to break into a few existing groups, only to have kids turn their backs on him and edge him out of their conversations. He would occasionally check his phone, most likely texting someone, anyone he knew that might be at the game. I watched this student go through rejection after rejection for most of the game until he finally found *one* friend he could stand with and pretend to care about the game.

When I talk to young adults today, they frequently talk about the Rejection Bag they have packed in some way for most of their life. Kids live with a fear of rejection. In one focus group, the first thing they talked about was the multiple ways they had felt rejected over the years. They talked about not having anywhere to fit in at school, struggling in dating, and having an overall sense that people are going to turn their back on them. Unfortunately, that's their experience.

As I've mentioned in several chapters, these bags often layer and overlap. The bag of rejection can be built on performance and identity baggage. If my performance isn't up to par and I get rejected because of that, I begin to see myself as a loser who can never live up to anything. If I consistently feel like I'm a loser who can never live up to anything, it just becomes part of my identity. It's who I am.

## *Rejection by Family*

When I first met Kurt, he was in his mid-twenties. He had grown up in church with a family that was always around ministry. He had moved to our town from another part of the country and had connected with a group of young adults that were emerging leaders in our church. Kurt and others from his crew were volunteering in the youth ministry and other areas of the church. He was a great guy who was striving to grow in his faith.

After a few years of being around Kurt in several different settings, we began to talk about the deeper issues of life. I suspected he was struggling with a major issue, and one day he invited me to lunch because he needed to talk. Over a few hours, he shared he was struggling with same-sex attraction, and it was a real battle. He didn't identify as homosexual, he had not acted on any of his thoughts, and he needed help. As we talked about his journey, I asked him about his family and if they knew. He said they did, and that's why he was in our town. He had been rejected by his family and he had been struggling with this burden on his own for years.

One focus group I led had two young adults in it who told particularly sad stories. One shared a story about his dad. He recalled a difficult family moment when there was a lot of tension and arguing. He remembers his dad saying to his mom, "I don't want these children." The young adult said, "He chose not to love me." Another young man in that same group opened up about his life. He has autism, ADD, and has struggled with depression. He said, "My parents never knew how to deal with me. I almost feel like my dad wants to get rid of me. I sometimes question if they have ever loved me." Although these are extreme situations, more people have thoughts and feelings like this than we care to admit.

There is perhaps no deeper pain than being rejected by one's family of origin. The bonds of love start so deep when we are young, and I believe we all desperately need acceptance from our family to be whole. I know of so many adults who feel some sense of rejection from their parents or siblings, and this rejection haunts them for the rest of their life. Many people learn to suppress and ignore this pain, but it's there, and it packs some of the hardest baggage to deal with.

# *Rejection by Teams/Groups/Organizations*

As tryouts started, I had my hopes up. Our son had been playing recreational baseball for a few years, and he enjoyed it. He was a good player; not great, but good. He wanted to play for the middle school team and, as an 8th grader, I thought he had a pretty good chance to make the roster. In the weeks leading up to tryouts, he had been working hard to get better. We would spend time in the yard throwing, and we made frequent trips to the batting cage. He was ready for the challenge.

I've never been one of those dads who stays to watch tryouts or practice, but this time I was really curious (and pulling for my son). For three days I arranged my work schedule so I could make it to school and watch the last hour of tryouts. I parked the car in a space where I could see the field and all that was going on while staying a comfortable distance from the action. As is the case with most try-outs, there seemed to be a group of kids who were definitely going to make the team, another group of kids who had no chance, and a huge pack in the middle. My son was in the middle. I did think he was close to the top of the middle bunch, but I might have been a little biased. As the days unfolded and I realized this might not work out for him, I felt a bit of sadness.

After the third day of tryouts, the coaches were going to post on-line who made the team. That night I must have refreshed the website thirty or forty times waiting to learn his fate. When I saw that he hadn't made it, my heart sank. I didn't say anything to him because he was checking the site too (although not as much as I was). When he saw that his number wasn't on the list, he quietly went to his room, not telling me or my wife. Sometime later he emerged, and we could tell what he was feeling from the look on his face.

A few years later a similar scenario played out with our daughter. Within the span of a few weeks, she got cut from the middle school basketball team and didn't make a travel team she wanted to join. When we told her about the travel team, she was kind of quiet. While shopping with my wife the next day, a burst of anger came out. They were finishing up at the mall and were stopping at a cookie stand to get a snack. My wife asked our daughter what she wanted. She said, "Give me a basketball cookie so I can smash it up in my mouth." The painful feelings of rejection were real.

This scenario and others like it play out in our homes all the time. It's not just with sports, but in other areas of life too. Our kids might not have the grades to get in the honor society or they may not get the part they want in the school play. They may not get the job they applied for. They may make a poor decision that gets them kicked out of something they are involved with. They may not be selected for an award or a scholarship. Facing rejection is unfortunately a part of life that we all must learn to navigate.

## Rejection by Friends and Peers

My wife still vividly remembers the day at school when her two best school friends flat out rejected her. There was one friend in particular whom she had idolized. She dressed like her, did her hair like her, even packed the same lunch as her. One day in 7th grade my wife walked up to these friends to join the conversation. They turned their backs on her and would not speak to her. She has no idea why, but that's what they did. To me, it sounds like classic *mean girl* behavior, and it's safe to say that my wife wasn't friends with them after that day. The rejection was real and hard to handle. She cried at school and then she went home and cried some more. But pretty quickly, she moved on. She had her neighborhood friends who didn't know her school friends. She had other school friends to whom she eventually grew closer. Summer soon came, and she didn't even see those two girls anymore. Good riddance if you ask me!

Situations like this one still occur, but rejection can be a lot harder for kids in this generation. Because of the internet and social media, kids and teens instantly see what they are missing, the party they weren't invited to, and the fun others are having without them. Posting a photo online and not getting as many likes as you want can feel like rejection. So many teenagers and young adults find their sense of worth in their online presence. Cyberbullying is a real thing that pushes kids to feel rejection deeply. It used to be that kids could come home to a haven and be protected from the world, but now the world and its hurtful ways are always at our kids' fingertips. Technology can be a beautiful thing, but it can also be incredibly harmful if we don't pay attention and harness it.

Rejection Baggage is closely tied to our ability to trust. One college student shared, "It can be very hard to go into a relationship with full trust of the other person if you have had relationships broken because of trust. Broken trust can make future relationships difficult because of the fear of trust being broken again. You constantly worry about the relationship and whether you should or can trust the person."

There is another layer to rejection that kids feel from their friends, and it's in their dating lives. When a couple spends time together building their relationship and creating a deep bond, the inevitable breakup produces a feeling of heartbreak (at least what they think is heartbreak). Teens and young adults often don't know how to process this pain and feelings of rejection and inadequacy can go incredibly deep. These situations are compounded when sexual activity has been a part of the relationship.

## The Burden of the Bag:
## What Happens if the Rejection Bag Gets Packed?

As with most of the bags, different kids react to things in different ways and not all kids experience the same pain. Based on what I have heard and seen over the years, I can give us a small snapshot of the ramifications of packing the Rejection Bag. If our kids pack this bag, they could:

- Have a hard time trusting people in general—When kids get rejected from people they are hoping will embrace them, it makes it incredibly difficult to trust anyone.

- Build a shell and tend to reject others as they move through life—When kids believe rejection is a normal part of life, they may begin to reject others themselves and/or use rejection as a defense mechanism.

- Struggle with loneliness—When kids experience rejection, they may tend to live more isolated lives and experience loneliness.

- Struggle in relationships—When there is a pattern of rejection, relationships may be harder to build and solidify.

- Develop low self-esteem—When kids and teens consistently feel like they are rejected, they struggle to have a healthy sense of self.

## Lightening the Load:
## Fighting the Rejection Bag

*Make sure your kids* **never** *feel rejected by you or your family.*

One of the things I want my kids to know beyond the shadow of a doubt is that I, as their father, accept them. This is critical for them as they develop their identity, especially during their elementary and teenage years. They have to not only know I love and accept them, but they have to *feel* it. As we navigate life and our daily routine, this can be tricky. There are times when I have to push them, challenge them, and discipline them. Sometimes in our discipline, they need to feel we are disappointed in them. But we need to make sure they *never* feel like we reject them.

As our children get older and start making more and more decisions, they can easily feel rejected by certain family members because of decisions they make or ideas they have. They may decide they don't quite buy into everything that mom and dad do, and they begin to develop opinions of their own. This can range from politics to sports teams to social issues, and even faith. As they have grown up, we have hopefully taught them to think for themselves and become more independent. Sadly, for a lot of kids, the family starts to shun them when they start to do the very thing we've trained them to do.

Not only do they start to form and express their own views and opinions, but their decisions can have greater and greater consequences. When a teenager or young adult makes a bad decision that gets them in real trouble, they need their family more than ever. While we do need to express our displeasure with the decisions they have made, we also need to do everything we can to stand *with* them and let them know we're there for them. We need to make sure that, in the times they need us the most, they feel loved and accepted by the people they are most looking to for that love and acceptance.

***When they are rejected by a team, group, or organization, help them process why and help them know how to improve.***

When my son didn't make the middle school baseball team, I had a choice to make as a dad. I was obviously going to let him know how much I love and believe in him. I also knew he just wasn't good enough to make the final cut. I asked him why he thought he didn't make it. He could identify a few things that probably held him back, but not everything.

So many kids have an unrealistic picture of their ability, especially in sports. How often do we hear elementary and middle school boys talk about how they are going to play a professional sport? Some will, but the vast majority won't. As parents, we *have* to be honest with ourselves and be honest with our kids about where they are when it comes to their talent. When they aren't quite good enough and don't make the team or get the grade, it is our job to help them see the truth and understand why. It's easy to blame the coach for not choosing them or the teacher for not teaching them but, when we do that, we contribute to the Authority Bag that our kids are already packing.

When our kids don't get a part in the play or don't make it into the honor society, the best thing we can do is help them to see how they need to improve. This can be tricky because we don't want to turn up the performance heat or make them feel as if they have to earn our support. But, if we're honest, we are often the best people to see where they can do better. If we can master the art of encouraging them in the right way, we can help them learn to accept the situation and work to be better the next time.

*When they are rejected by their peers, help them process why.*

For a season in our daughter's life, she was having a bit of a hard time figuring out how to navigate a few relationships. There was a great group of girls in our neighborhood that played together almost every day. There began to be rumblings of trouble, and some of the girls didn't want to play with my daughter because they said she could be "a bit bossy!" If I'm honest, we had some similar feelings and experiences at home. My wife and I had to learn how to both empathize with her feelings of mild rejection from the group while, at the same time, help her see there was a bit of truth to the situation. We wanted to help her grow and develop as a person and realize why there was relational tension with her friends. Part of why she may have been seen as "bossy" is because she is a leader, and we love that about her. We just needed to help her redirect her emerging leadership skills and use them in a healthy way that her friends could receive.

As your kids work through their relationships, pay attention to what is going on. Are certain friends fading away? Are there situations bothering your kids? Is there relational drama? This is tricky because we don't want to be the "helicopter parents" we've already discussed. But we do want to be aware if our kids are being rejected by their friends or if they are rejecting anyone. Be observant of how your kids are treating the other kids around them and, when you see them pushing others away, coach them in how they can change their mindset and hopefully not develop a pattern of rejecting others.

*When they are rejected, be more aware and be more present.*

Earlier in this chapter, I shared times when both my son and daughter didn't make the school teams they so eagerly wanted to be selected for. I often see my kids struggle relationally with friends and face challenges. If your kids are involved in activities at all, you can probably list times when they have been rejected. These are times when they may put on a tough outer shell and seem as if they don't need us. If we look closer and push in, we can see these are times when they may need us the most.

When you know that your kids have been rejected (from any-thing), make the effort to be especially present in their life, at least for a season. You may need to rearrange your schedule and be home for a few more hours than normal. Take them out for an impromptu dinner or ice cream. Don't make a big deal out of it, just be there. And don't force a conversation about their feelings of rejection. They might not be ready. Just show them how much you love and care for them and help them *feel* the acceptance they crave.

### *When they are rejected, remind them they are fully accepted by their Heavenly Father.*

It may not resonate in the moment, but when our kids are rejected by anyone or anything, they need to be reminded they will never be rejected by God. Hopefully, the foundation for this feeling comes from their belief they are loved and accepted by you. We know from Romans 3:23 that "all have sinned and fall short of the glory of God." We also know that God's grace covers any and everything, and forgiveness and acceptance into His family are open to all who believe. We need to remind our kids that God will never turn His back on them, and He will always love and be with them, even when they don't feel it.

### *When they are rejected, remind them of who and Whose they are.*

If you can help a rejected child or teen understand they are never rejected by God, the next step is reminding them their identity resides in their relationship with God, not their acceptance by anyone in the world. They are a child of God, loved by Him, and they can rest in

121

that identity. This intimately connects with the Identity Baggage we all struggle with. If someone can rest in their identity in Christ and learn how to live from that truth, rejection from people and organizations in the world might not hurt quite as much. This is obviously a journey for all of us, and rejection always hurts. But, if we can help our kids embrace their identity in Whose they are (God's) instead of who accepts them here on the earth, they can deal with rejection in a much healthier way.

### When they are rejected by their peers, help them connect with other friends.

Identify other kids you want your kids to be around and do your best to put them in situations where they can connect with these new friends. When kids are younger, organized play dates and family gatherings can facilitate relationships you want to foster. This takes effort and it helps if you as parents also relationally connect. This gets *much* harder as our kids get older. Teenagers don't usually take kindly to arranged friendships, but it can be done. Invite families over for dinner or organize outings. More time together can often breed a fondness that will lead to a real, authentic friendship.

Involvement in a local church can be a key piece of this strategy. Many churches organize kids and teens into small groups that meet together consistently. If your son or daughter is in a group, do what you can to meet and get to know the other kids in the group. Volunteer to host a gathering at your house or help out in some way at church. If you know who you can steer your kids to, it makes it much easier to make it happen.

### Monitor devices and social media.

If I'm honest, I hate that we live in a world where we have to monitor screen time for our kids, but we do. So many parents ask the question, "When is the right age to get my kid a phone?" In my opinion, there is no right answer to that question. I would encourage you to wait as long as you can and have limits, especially when they first get it. Once unlimited access is granted, it's really hard to go back. I would also encourage you not to let your kids have their devices in their rooms, especially at night. If they do, they will be on it until the wee hours of the morning, lose sleep, and get sucked into the endless world of scrolling. They can't stop themselves. The more they are on the device, the more opportunity they have to feel inadequate and rejected in so many ways. As we've already talked about, "You have to be where they are." I came across this idea when researching a seminar I was leading on helping our kids navigate technology and social media. Several different ministries and organizations used some version of this statement and encouraged parents to closely follow their kids online. I have come to totally ascribe to this philosophy. I believe it, not because I see what my kids are posting online, but because I have seen what other kids, teens, and young adults are posting. I don't follow a ton of kids, but there are a few family friends and kids from church I do follow. You can learn a lot about someone based on what photos they share with the world, things they like, or on what they comment.

I understand the idea that our kids need some semblance of privacy, but the mere fact they are choosing to be on *social media* and share with the world, I think it's only reasonable that I, as one of the people who brought them into the world, have the right to see what they share. I don't have to constantly question them on their online presence, but there may be times when I can sense a pattern, especially when it comes to how they are being treated online or how they are treating others. If we know that a rise in social media and the importance of "likes" is contributing to our kids' feelings of rejection, anxiety, and depression, it only makes sense that we pay attention to what is happening online with our kids.

## Wrapping up the Rejection Bag

Dave really was a great kid. He was smart, funny, somewhat quiet, and overall easy to like. He got invited to be a part of the church youth group by a few football players who were already involved. He joined us on Sunday nights, went on a few retreats and mission trips, and participated in weekly Bible studies. He seemed to be growing in confidence and learning about Christian faith.

For a few weeks, I noticed that Dave was no longer coming around. His parents weren't a part of our church and I didn't even know them. I started to ask some of his friends why Dave wasn't coming anymore, and they seemed a bit uncomfortable with my line of questioning. This was in the early 2000s at the beginning of the rise of social media, and teenagers were just beginning to create profiles and swim in this pond. I decided to dig a little deeper into what was going on. After a few days, I found out that some kids at school had created a social media account for Dave, without his knowledge. They came up with an insulting username that resembled his full name. He was a bit of a large kid, so the name they created made fun of his size. For several weeks, they posted pictures and quotes making fun of Dave. It was a classic case of cyberbullying.

When I finally got a hold of him to talk about the situation, Dave was embarrassed. He felt rejected by his so-called friends and he was incredibly hurt. He had retreated from almost everyone, and he felt all alone in his pain. I tried hard to comfort him, let him know how much we loved him, and how we wanted to help him walk through his pain. He said, "maybe" but I never really got to spend any significant time with Dave again. From what I watched from afar for the next few years, he really struggled processing his rejection baggage. He dealt with anxiety and depression, and he seemed to have a hard time fitting in anywhere. Looking at his social media now (20 years later), he still seems to be a hurting puppy. I have no idea if Dave's parents ever knew about what went on, but I do wonder if there could have been some way they could have better helped him work through the pain.

As I've thought through this concept of baggage for the last several years, I've known that all of what we pack leads to some level of anxiety. The rise of anxiety that leads to depression in our world is heartbreaking. We see so many kids, teens, and adults struggle in these areas. I have come to believe that the bag of rejection, which leads someone to question their worth, is one of the biggest contributors to the anxiety and depression people feel. This bag can come with a lot of "extras." One young adult told me, "You need to understand the fear of rejection before you get rejected. That bag of rejection can have a lot more bags piled into it."

As parents, we are never going to be able to protect our kids from experiencing rejection. It will be a part of life (and maybe a big one). We can, however, help them learn how to minimize the pain of rejection and build a healthy sense of self in a world that will almost always let them down. Rejection is painful and we often suffer because of it. But, we need to remember Scripture tells us that pain and suffering, if we reframe it, can be an important part of our spiritual growth. God can use evil and suffering for good. In Genesis 37, Joseph was sold into slavery by his brothers who rejected him. But God used evil for good by eventually elevating Joseph and using him in mighty ways. Because of his trust, perseverance, and understanding of who he was, Joseph was able to work through his rejection.

Romans 5:3-5 says, "Not only so, but we also glory in our suffer-ings, because we know that suffering produces perseverance; perse-verance, character; and character, hope. And hope does not put us to shame, because God's love has been poured out into our hearts through the Holy Spirit, who has been given to us."

If we help our kids develop a solid foundation of identity and trust, if we pay attention to the rejection that comes their way, and if we help them move through their rejection in healthy ways, we can help them minimize the Rejection Baggage they carry and live lives free from the deep pain this bag produces. We can help them develop a spirit of hope that helps them push away the shame they feel through rejection. They can live from their identity in Christ rather than from any acceptance they feel like they need from the world.

## *Reflection Questions*

How have you struggled with the pain of rejection over your life-time? What are some ways you have dealt with this pain?

Are there things you unintentionally do to make your kids feel like they have been rejected by you? What can you do to help them know they are accepted by you no matter what?

Has there been a time when your kids experienced rejection from a team or organization? How did or could you help them process this pain? When your kids are rejected by a team or organization for a legitimate reason, how can you help them self-evaluate and improve the skill or talent they are hoping to develop?

Has there been a time when your kids were rejected by their peers? What are some things you did or could do to help them process this pain and feel accepted? Do you ever see your child participating in rejecting their peers? If so, how can you help them be more compassionate and learn to truly accept others?

As your kids experience rejection in life (which they will), how can you remind them to embrace their identity in Christ and live under the truth that they are accepted by God?

## Chapter Eight

# The Guilt and Shame Bag

*"Shame just feeds itself. I don't talk about it, and I leave it in the dark."—young adult*

As I sat in the focus group with this group of young men, they kind of talked in code for a while. It was clear they all resonated with my questions about baggage, and I think most of their minds went to the same place. One young man finally said, "It really is all about mental impurity and lust. We struggle with what the world says, what my body's biology says, and what God says. I'm not walking that line very well." So many kids are struggling with God's design for sexuality and marriage. They've been taught all about it in the church, but they sometimes just don't buy-in. As children grow into teens and young adults, their sexual struggles and the decisions they make quickly start to haunt them.

The young man continued, "The shame of past thoughts and actions makes you feel like you are incapable of getting into line with God's design." Others in the room were nodding their heads. Did you hear that? Because of their baggage, they feel incapable of living the life God has designed them to live. They feel like the battle is already over. They have heard God can overcome anything, and they can be "made new" again, but they struggle to embrace the real grace of God and live in the freedom that grace offers. I recently met with a young adult who desperately wants to live a life that is honoring God, but his feelings and emotions about relationships and sexuality rule his mind and heart. You can see the burden he carries in his eyes. The next bag is the Guilt and Shame Bag, and it often revolves around sex, lust, and bad decisions in this area of life.

Guilt and shame can begin to take root in our lives at an early age. I can remember taking change off my dad's dresser when I was a kid and putting it in my piggy bank (Okay, I was stealing). While something in me (oh, maybe sin?) pushed me to keep doing it, something else in me knew it was wrong and made me feel bad. I felt guilty for what I had done, and shame followed me around even though I'm pretty sure my parents were unaware of my "get rich quick" plan.

As we step into this bag, I do want to acknowledge there is a real difference between guilt and shame. There is a lot of writing on this subject, and I agree the two are distinctively different. Guilt can actually be helpful and move us to a different line of thinking and behavior. Shame, on the other hand, leads us to feel unworthy and somehow flawed as a person. For this chapter, I want to couple them together because that's often what we do in our parenting. The guilt we as adults sometimes use and our kids feel is often linked to the shame produced in them. I recognize that most of the real baggage that comes from this part of the conversation is rooted in shame. I do think guilt is a close cousin in this context.

The guilt and shame bag can honestly be one of the heaviest for someone to carry, and it takes a lot of work to overcome. Helping our kids *not* pack this one bag may be worth the entire read of this book. In our pre-marital counseling, it is often obvious this bag can be a tremendous barrier in relationships, especially when past decisions around sex are involved. Past sexual encounters and pornography are two of the greatest culprits leading to shame among adolescents. The average age of first exposure to pornography is around age eleven. My wife remembers her first exposure to pornography at a friend's house when she was in middle school. She and her friend found a stack of Playboy magazines under her friend's parent's bed. This is probably pretty typical for our generation's exposure to pornography, but it is a whole new ball game in the digital age.

On their website *Fight the New Drug* puts it this way: "Honestly, parents—elementary aged kids and teens in the world today are facing issues that you and your parents never even imagined when you were growing up. When a lot of today's parents were young, if anyone wanted porn, they had to look pretty hard in order to get their hands on it. They'd go to the local store and have to show their ID, and actually ask a store clerk for that magazine. Fast forward a few years, and today's children can consume limitless amounts of it with one click of a mouse or tap on a screen. It's increasingly more hardcore, and increasingly more available than ever."[1]

One of the scariest things we as parents have to grapple with is how easy it is for our kids to be exposed to pornography without even looking for it. Mistype a word in a search engine or on YouTube, and you might be surprised what can turn up. Like a particular photo on an app, and you are flooded with ads and photos you were not looking for. Follow a certain celebrity or one of your friends, and there is no telling what images and ideas that person may share. We all have to deal with this as adults and we struggle. Imagine what this is doing in the minds and hearts of our kids and teens.

*Fight the New Drug* also informs us of this: "More than 90% of all teenagers ages 12 to 17 have been exposed to hardcore pornography, and once they've been exposed, many keep coming back. It's no longer a question of *if* your child will be exposed to pornographic material online, but *when*. It's up to parents to instill their family values backed by research into their child's mindset."[2]

One theme I've seen for over 25 years in my role as a pastor is the pain of all kinds of shame. If we go back to the beginning of time (the Garden of Eden), the first response to sin was shame. When Adam and Eve ate from the tree of the knowledge of good and evil, Genesis 3:7 says "the eyes of both of them were opened, and they realized they were naked; so they sewed fig leaves together and made coverings for themselves." They were ashamed and began to hide who they were. When God was looking for them in the garden, "they hid from the Lord God among the trees of the garden." Because of their choices, they began to pack some guilt and shame baggage that we have all been dealing with since.

While we develop a ton of guilt and shame around our sexual thoughts and experiences, we also accumulate this baggage in other ways. Guilt and shame often get heaped on us from others. Parents, teachers, coaches, siblings, and peers all subtly (or intentionally) use guilt and shame to motivate, discipline, or manipulate us, and sometimes it works. People get what they want out of us by guilting or shaming us into certain behaviors or decisions, so they keep using that strategy.

For so many kids in society today, they are dealing with the shame of a family they wish was different, and this has so many layers. Children of divorce often wonder what role they played in their parents' breakup. I can't tell you how many times I've heard some version of, "I thought I was the reason they divorced." Even though many parents who go through a divorce go to great lengths to let their kids know they aren't the reason, the question still lingers. Kids can feel abandoned and worthless, especially girls. The guilt and shame can feed a never-ending cycle that plays into rejection and comparison. Kids begin to look around and believe, "I'm not like that kid with that family."

There are several reasons why this bag can so easily get packed, especially for kids, teens, and young adults. Studies have taught us that a person's brain is not fully developed until they are in their late 20s and possibly their early 30s. Young people are simply not consistently able to healthily process what is happening to them as they grow up being made to feel guilt and shame. They need someone to talk to about how they are feeling, and that avenue rarely exists. Kids who grow up in homes where parents avoid wading into the real conversations are simply stuffing their emotions deep down inside and packing some tremendous bags. When our kids make mistakes, our parenting strategy spirals into "go to your room" or "you're grounded" instead of talking through the situation and ultimately offering forgiveness.

One college student shared, "I had a lot of shame. There were a lot of things that I struggled with in my faith and my walk with God. I had the 'perfect family' so I couldn't process my thoughts and decisions with my parents."

One young adult said, "There is lots of shame that no one knows about. It pushes us to build up walls, and we're scared to let anyone in so they see who we really are." When the topic of guilt and shame came up in one focus group, someone said, "It keeps people crippled."

Being more exposed to the issues of today throws kids into shame and isolation. Kids will stuff down their feelings because they have no one to talk with. The key relationships in their lives aren't strong enough to support the weight of the conversations they need to have.

One young adult shared, "I wanted to talk to my mom about things, but I would get a lecture every time. I really wanted to tell her about stuff, but I didn't want an argument. I just wanted to express my feelings." This young lady was craving a conversation. She needed support. She was dying inside and needed the love of a mother, but what she felt was the criticism of a parent who wanted to try solving a problem and bring her daughter in line.

This points to the importance of relationships, but we've already talked about that. As parents, we often don't have the capacity ourselves to have a healthy conversation, so we revert to "lecture" or "fix it" mode. It's just easier. When we don't empathize with our children and lean into a real, loving, healthy conversation with them about what is going on in their lives, the shame they feel goes deeper and deeper into their psyche. They become more and more hurt, confused, sad, and anxious. They are crying out for help, and we aren't listening.

The Guilt and Shame Bag can easily have a direct relationship to the Identity Bag. As kids grow up feeling bad about what they have done, they easily transfer that into thinking this is who they are. The idea that "I am what I do" is real and can push kids into repeated destructive behavior unless they have somewhere to process the truth of who God has created them to be, even when they mess up.

One more thing. As more and more troubling things happen in our society, there is often shame that kids feel not about what they have done, but what has been done to them. Sexual assault, bullying, and online shaming continue to be unfortunate parts of living in this world. These are a parent's worst nightmare. We need to become aware of the signs of sexual abuse, bullying, and shaming, and learn how to safeguard our children from these real threats to their physical, mental, emotional, and spiritual health. As we pay attention to what is happening to our kids, we have to treat these situations with extra caution. Many of the suggestions I'll offer in the coming pages can possibly help when kids experience the pain of someone violating them in some way. But often these deeper wounds will need the help of a professional to move toward real healing. This book is essentially about preventative maintenance when it comes to packing bags, so we hope to stop these situations from ever happening.

## The Burden of the Bag:
## What Happens if the Guilt and Shame Bag Gets Packed?

Guilt and Shame Baggage can lead kids into an overwhelming spiral of feelings and emotions that are too much to deal with here. Based on what I have heard and seen over the years, I can give us a small snapshot of the ramifications of packing the guilt and shame bag. If our kids pack the guilt and shame bag, they could:

- Have a defeated sense of self and build a destructive identity—When guilt and shame rule the day in a kid or teen's thoughts, they may feel defeated and begin to live into the identity this baggage produces.

- Question whether or not they can ever get out of sinful patterns—When kids never learn how to deal with their shame in a healthy way and get to redemption, they are likely to stay in destructive patterns.

- Struggle with making romantic relational connections—When anyone carries guilt and shame about sexual thoughts, choices, or events, that pain carries into new romantic relationships and creates a barrier to real connections.

- Struggle with believing God can forgive them for what they have done—When the cycle of guilt and shame takes root

135

and kids struggle to forgive themselves, they have a hard time believing God can forgive them.

- Tend to shut down and stuff things inside—When there is no one to talk to and no way to process the guilt and shame they feel, kids can tend to shut down, isolate, and internalize everything.

- See themselves as the problem—When kids are ashamed and constantly carry guilt, they can begin to believe there is something wrong with them and they are the problem.

## Lightening the Load:
## Fighting the Guilt and Shame Bag

*Don't use guilt and shame as a parenting tool.*

We've all been there. Our kids do something wrong and we want them to know exactly how bad it was. We use the words, "You should be ashamed of yourself." We're trying to make them feel guilty for what they have done and turn from their ways. The problem is that our kids listen to us and they do feel ashamed, but not just for the transgression. They simply feel ashamed of who they are. The guilt we use pushes them to a shame they feel, and it all seeps into their identity.

Do everything you can *not* to use guilt and shame as a parenting tool. Our kids do need to know we are disappointed when they disobey or make poor decisions. We just need to do our best *not* to develop a pattern of shaming them into "doing the right thing." Not only will they not own the idea they should be making better decisions, but they will also develop a mindset they are not worthy of our love unless they can earn it. If we're not careful, we can pack a relational performance bag at the same time.

***Help them know that no matter what they do, they are loved and forgiven by God and by you.***

In those times when our kids screw up, we need to make sure they know they are forgiven. We often try to do this with our words, but I think our kids need more than that. We need to make sure they not only hear they are forgiven, but they need to feel like they are forgiven. As mentioned in an earlier chapter, I remember being encouraged by a friend who was ahead of me in parenting to always "restore the relationship" after a fight with one of my kids. Most often our fights revolve around us trying to discipline our children and correct them for what they have done wrong. I can remember nights when I would go into one of our kids' rooms and talk with them after a big fight. I was pretty relentless in trying to make them smile, laugh, and hug me before I left. I never wanted to let the distance that had been created between us be the last thing they thought about when they went to sleep. I wanted them to know I forgave them, and they did not need to feel guilt and shame. I often needed their forgiveness too.

This idea has an even bigger implication when it comes to our kids' faith. If they don't feel forgiven by us, how can they trust they are forgiven by God? As parents (especially dads), we are a physical representation of a heavenly Father who loves and forgives us. God does not want us, His children, to live with guilt and shame, and so we need to help our children understand this truth. One of the main ways our kids will believe God can and will forgive them for their mistakes is if they believe we do.

***Help them know they are not defined by their choices and actions.***

So many of the bags kids pack can overlap. As kids grow up and struggle with the mistakes they have made and the shame they feel, they can easily come to believe they are defined by their sin and the poor choices they have made. They need to know their identity is

137

*not* a sum of their bad choices. As parents, we need to help them see this. Romans 8:1 says, "Therefore, there is now no condemnation for those who are in Christ Jesus." Our kids need to know that, deep in their souls.

As with many of my encouragements, this one starts with you as their leader. You need to know, feel, and live the truth that you are not defined by your past actions. The shame you feel for your decisions can be covered, and you can be renewed in your life. If your kids see, hear, and feel you wallowing in shame from a past life, it will be incredibly hard for them to overcome the pain of their shame. Modeling this for your kids can go a long way toward helping them not deal with this incredibly painful baggage.

### *Talk to them about pornography and sex.*

I know these can be uncomfortable subjects to talk about with your kids, but if they aren't getting information from you, I can promise you they are getting it from somewhere or someone else. We have to be willing to keep gently knocking on the door of our kids' hearts and be ready to step into these conversations when the door opens. I'm not talking about giving them stats about teenage pregnancy or trying to scare them about what it means to parent a human. Talk to them about their emotions and feelings, their thoughts and desires. Help them understand that God created sex and He intends for it to be good in the context of marriage. Talk to them about the benefits of waiting and the pain that comes with poor choices. Talk to them about objectification and addiction and do it all without a judgmental tone. We've all struggled in this area in some way, so let your kids know you are there to help them navigate this difficult journey.

The following websites have good resources for how to have these discussions with your kids:

- https://fightthenewdrug.org/the-guideline-how-to-talk-to-your-kids-about-porn/
- http://thenovusproject.org/resource-hub/parents

***Help them know they are not responsible for what has happened to them, and they can live a life free from the pain of the past.***

As I mentioned at the beginning of this chapter, some kids, teens, and young adults today are victims of absolutely terrible things. Due to no fault of their own, they are experiencing tremendous emotional pain, suffering, and shame because of what has been done to them. In these situations, there is a chance there may be some feelings of guilt or shame baggage that follows them around for the rest of their lives if they don't get the right help. As their parents, you can hopefully help them mitigate this pain and baggage by helping them see and believe they are *not* responsible for what has happened to them. Just like we can be forgiven for choices we've made and sins we've committed, we can be equally washed clean for sins others have committed against us. Even though victims don't need forgiveness in any way, they often feel like they do. Part of our job is to love and encourage them in such a way the deeper bags of shame don't take root. If we're honest, helping our kids with this kind of baggage is out of our league. If your child, teen, or young adult is walking through a journey like this, please get them trauma-informed professional help.

A friend who is a survivor of sexual abuse, author on the subject, and founder of a great ministry helping women find healing and hope in Jesus shared this with me: "I was set free from feelings of guilt and shame as I learned the truth about sexual abuse, about who God is and who I am in Christ, and about what it takes to heal. I now know the abuse was not my fault in any way, and because of this and Jesus,

I have lived shame free for years. When a victim/survivor is properly educated on the truth about abuse, has a safe place to tell their story with safe people who understand, and are continually affirmed they are in no way at fault, the victim/survivor will ultimately, over time, receive that truth in their heart as reality. Add the Gospel in there, and you have a recipe for shame-free living. I've seen this at work in many of the women (and men) we serve in our ministry."

*Darkness to Light* (www.D2L.org), and *The Mama Bear Effect* (www.themamabeareffect.org) are two great resources for parents helping their kids navigate these issues. Both are excellent places for parents to start becoming aware of the issues. *Darkness to Light* is a nationally respected child advocacy effort that helps adults understand their role in protecting kids from child sexual abuse. *The Mama Bear Effect* teaches parents how to talk about body safety and boundaries in age-appropriate ways, to help empower children and parents with truth and wisdom on this issue and how to prevent it in their family.

### Build a relationship that allows you to be able to talk to them when they make poor choices and feel guilt and shame.

I've devoted an entire chapter to the importance of building our relationships with our kids, so I'm guessing you get the point. But, in the context of helping them navigate the guilt and shame they feel, it's worth talking about again. We need to have the kind of relationship with our kids where they are willing to share with us and let us in. We want them to let us know how they are thinking and how they see themselves. Because of their natural resistance, this is so hard. In chapter two, I cited something our pastor encourages parents with often: "Talk to them about everything so you can talk to them about anything." Do whatever you can to keep the lines of communication open so they might step into a healthy conversation. If we can be aware of what our kids are thinking, who they are around, and the direction they are heading, we can steer them away from situations where they might develop some real shame for their decisions. If they don't feel like they have a relationship with us where they can safely talk, we have little or no chance of helping them stay away from decisions that will produce guilt and shame.

We all know we will never be able to keep our kids from experiencing some sort of guilt and shame. Simply experiencing guilt and shame does not automatically lead someone to pack those bags. Getting rid of guilt and shame often starts with confession, and we want our home to be a safe place where our kids can confess their sin, feel forgiveness, and move on with life. When they have nowhere to confess, process, or experience forgiveness (from both us and God), they are in danger of packing some really heavy bags.

## Wrapping up the Guilt and Shame Bag

I first spent time with Javi when we were in an ordination group together. I had been ordained before, but my church wanted me to go through the process to get recognized in my new context. From what I had heard, he was an incredible guy. Boy was that true. Javi is now one of the pastors at our church and a great friend. He and his wife Lauren have three beautiful kids, and we love the time we get to spend with them. Occasionally in conversations, Javi's wife Lauren will talk about his "pre-Jesus" life. They got married after Javi had made a turn in his life and decided to follow Jesus. I don't know a ton about his previous life, but I know he had a daughter. She is in and out of Javi and Lauren's family today, and it's encouraging to see how he treats her as a dad. I also know he made some decisions he is not proud of and, because of those, he continues to work through some real guilt and shame.

One thing I love about Javi is the way he shares about the redemption of his past. He never glorifies the old days or seems to want to head back there. He just talks about the love and redemption of Jesus. His kids hear these stories and they know their dad is thankful for what God has done in his life. As they get older and can understand more, I believe the way Javi talks about what God has done for him will have a profound impact on his kids. They will see their dad, resting in the arms of Jesus and trusting that God can use his past.

When I think about a consistent way to help our kids not pack the guilt and shame bag, I think about redemption. The God of the universe has redeemed us all from sin and death through the sacrifice of his son on the cross. The resurrection of Jesus overcame sin and death, and that redemption story can be ours if we embrace it. As parents, we need to be all about telling stories of redemption. We need to let our kids know that the guilt, shame, and pain of past decisions can be redeemed. We can experience freedom from these bags through a real relationship with Jesus.

Unfortunately, there is not a lot of vulnerability in our homes or in the church. Because we as adults try to hide the pain and shame we feel, our kids develop a pattern of doing the same. They do learn from us. One young adult told us, "I never knew what my parents struggled with, so when I struggled, I felt shame." We have to learn how to be authentically and appropriately real with our kids as they grow up so they will come to understand we all deal with guilt and shame. The key is learning how to process it so it doesn't produce bags that are too heavy to carry.

As I talked to college students and young adults about the bag of guilt and shame, we often gravitated toward talking about identity. I've already mentioned the relationship these bags have. As adolescents move through life and try on different identities, they often learn they can't live up to the identity they seek. If they identify as a volleyball player but are not quite good enough, they feel shame. If they step into online gaming but can never figure it out, they feel shame. If they have been dreaming of getting into a particular college but get rejected, not only do they pack rejection baggage, but they pack shame bags as well. In each of these situations, they also pack some performance baggage, but we've already been there. The way these bags overlap is sobering.

So, where does our identity come from? How can we work through the guilt and shame we feel as we move through the decisions of life? For me, it all comes down to the redeeming power of Jesus and the life I can live in Him. Romans 5:1 tells us this: "Therefore, since we have been justified through faith, we have peace with God through our Lord Jesus Christ." There it is again: the peace with God that we all seek. If we have faith in God through Jesus, we are justified from our sin, and our guilt and shame can be washed away. We can be free of the bags that weigh us down and have real peace with God. If we, as parents, can embrace this truth, then we can hopefully pass it on to our kids. We can help them stay away from developing Guilt and Shame Baggage that has the potential to haunt them for the rest of their life.

## *Reflection Questions*

What are some ways you have experienced guilt and shame in your life? How does your experience with guilt and shame flow into your family dynamic?

Is the culture of your home one where your kids feel comfortable sharing what is going on in their lives and mistakes they have made?

How do you react when your child makes a mistake? What changes can you make to create a healthier environment?

If your child is an appropriate age, have you had conversations about sexual boundaries and pornography? If you know or sense that your child is struggling with sexual choices or pornography, how can you help them live a life of sexual integrity and get past the guilt and shame of the choices they have made?

How did your parents react to the big mistakes you made in life? Was their reaction helpful? What did you need in that moment and how might you provide what your kids need in their moments?

Have you ever used guilt and shame as a parenting tool? How can you handle these moments differently?

Is there anything you need to forgive your child for that you haven't already? How can you make sure your child feels that forgiveness?

**Endnotes**

[1] *Fight the New Drug,* https://fightthenewdrug.org/the-guideline-how-to-talk-to-your-kids-about-porn/).

[2] Ibid.

*Chapter Nine*

# The Disappointment Bag

*"We just don't know how to deal with disappointment."*
*—young adult*

Mary is a college student who I've known for a few years. She and her family have been involved in our church for a long time, and we would call them friends. In middle and high school, Mary seemed to have it all together. She was a good athlete who was on the school teams, she worked hard in school and got good grades, she had a lot of friends, and she was deeply involved with our youth group. She is one of those people who always has a smile on their face—really. On the surface, all looked good. From my perspective, Mary may have had it kind of easy as she grew up. There was never any real-life trauma that came her way. She has an amazing family, and I know her parents always tried to put her and her siblings in the best position to succeed, and they usually did. Life was good.

Mary got into a great college and headed off to the next phase of her life. Toward the end of her first semester away, I got a message from her. She didn't want to talk, but she wanted to text. She needed to get something off her chest, and my wife and I had somehow earned her trust over the years. She shared she was struggling with anxiety and depression and, because of that, she was ashamed. She didn't want anyone else to know because she was scared about how people would react or what they would think. She said, "It's so hard to admit it and be vulnerable about it." She was in a tough spot and was asking for help.

I was a bit shocked. Mary? Really? I couldn't imagine what would have pushed this bright, fun, successful young lady to a place of despair. As I thought about the semester she had just been through, it dawned on me. It was hard. There were many circumstances in the world and in her town that made being in college tough. I know she struggled to build new friendships, school was difficult, and her connection to God and church had faded. It seemed like, for the first time in her life, she was facing some real-world disappointment and she didn't know what to do. As I thought about Mary's story, I couldn't help but reflect on many similar stories I have heard over the years.

As I moved deeper and deeper into this project and talked to more and more college students and young adults, this bag seemed to gain more traction. It's not a bag they talk about a lot, but the pain of it slips out every so often. *It's a bag of disappointment.*

From the title of this bag, one might think it is a bag filled with disappointments kids have endured. But it is actually a little different. There are two main parts or layers to this bag:

- Kids have a hard time knowing how to deal with disappointment.
- Kids struggle with feeling like they *are* a disappointment.

Through talking with students, I have come to realize the problem is not that kids are packing a bag full of disappointments, but instead, they have had to face fewer disappointments than many of

146

us did growing up. In fact, some of them are finding themselves ill-equipped to deal with disappointment when it comes their way because they have dealt with so little real disappointment throughout their life. It's Mary's story. In addition, some of them have packed this bag with the feelings of *being* a disappointment and not measuring up.

## The Lawnmower Parent

When our small children fall and scrape their knees, we often swoop them up and cover them with kisses letting them know we love them and they are going to be okay. When our child doesn't make the team or get a part in the play, we take them out to get ice cream and console them. We have a natural tendency as parents to comfort our children when they are hurting, and this is a good thing. I've even advocated for some of these things in earlier chapters. But, is it possible for us to take it too far? Can we, as parents, get so involved in our kids' lives that we shield them from dealing with disappointment in a way that they never learn to navigate life on their own? Most of us have heard the term "helicopter parents" referring to parents who hover, are overprotective, and are over-involved in helping their children sort out problems. In the last several years, a new trend in parenting has been identified where parents essentially pave the way for their kids. These parents have been called "snowplow" or "lawnmower" parents. An anonymous post on www.weareteachers.com titled, "Lawnmower Parents Are the New Helicopter Parents & We Are Not Here for It" discusses this new trend. "Lawnmower parents go to whatever lengths necessary to prevent their child from having to face adversity, struggle, or failure. Instead of preparing children for challenges, they mow obstacles down so kids won't experience them in the first place."[1]

The writer of the article was a teacher, and she cited an example where she was called to the office to retrieve something for one of her students during her planning period. She assumed it was something like money or an inhaler. Instead, it was a water bottle. The father, somewhat embarrassedly, said his daughter continuously texted him saying she had to have the water bottle even though there are water fountains available at the school. The writer goes on to say that, while most people can empathize with why parents don't want to watch their child struggle, "We are creating a generation that has no idea what to do when they actually encounter struggle. A generation who panics or shuts down at the mere idea of failure. A generation for whom failure is far too painful, leaving them with coping mechanisms like addiction, blame, and internalization."[2]

It's one thing to bring a water bottle to your child at school on your way to work, but some of the other stories I have heard make me cringe. Recently I heard a story of a parent contacting a coach at a local university complaining about their child's playing time. My wife says she would have been mortified if her parents had ever contacted her high school coach about playing time—or about anything. When she sat on the bench her first couple of years on the team, it was because she knew the older players, and even some her age, were better than she was. By the time she was a senior, she was a starter. Having to wait and earn her spot taught her resilience and the importance of hard work. Many times, my father wanted to talk to my high school football coach about my playing time, but every time I was the one who told him "No way!"

I also know of parents who requested a meeting with their daughter's boyfriend's parents when the couple was going through a rough spot and even after the couple broke up. The kids were seniors in high school. As I mentioned in an earlier chapter, I've heard stories of parents wanting to come with adult children to job interviews or request to talk to the boss about benefits for their child. I frequently rhetorically ask myself, "What in the world are we doing to these kids?"

In the *Pittsburgh Mom Collective* blog[3], a mom and college professor gives some insight into the consequences lawnmowing parenting can have on our children. Lawnmower parenting can lead kids to be poorly equipped to deal with routine growing and learning experiences. This includes everything from having simple conversations with adults about everyday topics to dealing with difficult issues with their peers. When kids don't have the opportunities to make decisions on their own without the guidance of others, they become unable to make any decisions at all. As they move through their teenage years, kids whose parents pave the way lose their internal drive and constantly wonder if they have what it takes to accomplish anything on their own. If the road is not paved for them, they wonder if they can even be trusted to take the journey.

Ouch! This really does put things into perspective. For us to help our children grow into independent young adults, we have to let them fail. We have to let them work through problems and issues. We have to let them experience disappointment. For many of them, they cannot truly feel hurt and pain. Going deeper and deeper into a virtual world doesn't help. They don't know how to be and feel uncomfortable in the real world. I have seen this with my own kids. We need to walk them through pain and teach them to learn how to cope. Instead of fixing it ourselves, we need to develop the discipline to let them work through what is in front of them.

## *A Reminder to Parents*

None of us like to see our children struggle. None of us want to see our children hurting. But the truth is there is purpose in suffering and disappointment. Scripture tells us that suffering and trials are a part of life. Not only are they a part of life, but they are also a purposed part of our life. Sarah Young, in her devotional book *Jesus Calling*, writing from Jesus' perspective, puts it this way: "If you have the world's peace—everything going your way—you don't seek My unfathomable Peace. Thank Me when things do not go your way, because spiritual blessings come wrapped in trials. Adverse circumstances are normal in a fallen world. Expect them each day. Rejoice in the face of hardship, *for I have overcome the world.*"[4]

James 1:2-4 states, "Consider it pure joy, my brothers and sisters, whenever you face trials of many kinds, because you know that the testing of your faith produces perseverance. Let perseverance finish its work so that you may be mature and complete, not lacking anything."

While none of us enjoys trials or experiencing disappointment, I think many of us can attest it was during these times we have felt closest to God. Scripture promises us that God can, and does, bring something good out of every situation and He has a purpose for our difficult times. I often have to remember this for myself and remind myself to teach this to my children.

## *Feeling Like a Disappointment*

Because of what I heard from so many college students and young adults in so many focus groups, this became one of the saddest parts of this project for me. It can easily be summed up in this statement from a young man: "I was afraid to disappoint my parents. I'm still wanting their approval." A tremendous number of adolescents travel through their formative years feeling like they *are* a disappointment. They have not measured up. They have not achieved enough. They are not smart enough. They don't work hard enough. They aren't pretty enough. They are just not enough—and they don't believe they ever will be. This sentiment not only makes me sad; it makes them sad too. You can see it in their eyes. Their lack of confidence in themselves and their lack of hope in the future can often be traced back to the idea they aren't enough.

We have to acknowledge that our kids sometimes feel this from us. We may make them feel this way on purpose in order to get some point across. I'm not sure if this strategy is a good one, for many reasons. Most often, we make them feel this way unintentionally. Our subtle comments and actions over time lead them to build a story where they have disappointed us and they, therefore, are a disappointment. Once this movie starts in their head, it's hard to rewind.

We aren't the only ones feeding this disappointment narrative. They feel it from coaches, teachers, peers, and the culture they live in. If at practice they constantly hear criticism because they can't make the shot or they don't understand the concepts, they know they are disappointing their coach. If they can't quite get their lines down for their part in the play, they know they are disappointing the director. When their body doesn't live up to the images they see on social media, they disappoint themselves.

So many of the other bags contribute to this one. Feeling like a disappointment can stem from rejection, performance, comparison, and shame. Our job, as parents, is to pay attention to the root of their disappointment and help them deal with it in a healthy way.

## The Burden of the Bag:
## What Happens if the Disappointment Bag Gets Packed?

There can and will be consequences if our kids never learn to deal with disappointment or if they feel like they are a disappointment to others and that feeling defines who they are. I've touched on a few of these consequences already, but if kids pack the disappointment bag they may:

- Be unequipped when disappointment comes their way—When kids and teens have never experienced real disappointment, they are blindsided when they become college students or young adults and find that disappointment is a regular part of life.

- Fail to recognize when it is their fault or they are in the wrong—When kids, teens, and young adults haven't felt disappointment in their decisions and haven't had to deal with many consequences, they may be blind to poor decisions they make and how those decisions impact others.

- Have a hard time believing in themselves and pushing themselves—When their childhood has consisted of feeling like a failure and disappointment, they may not believe they can ever achieve anything good and fail to work hard to do so.

- Struggle to believe they will ever be enough in relationships, particularly dating ones—When adolescents and young adults feel like they constantly disappoint others, they may shy away from significant romantic relationships for fear of experiencing or being a disappointment yet again. Worse yet, they may find themselves in relationships where they are taken advantage of because they don't believe in their self-worth.

- Tend to isolate and hide because they feel like they will again be a disappointment—When people feel like they will always feel the pain of experiencing disappointment or disappointing others, they may isolate themselves from others and become lonely. It's just easier.

## Lightening the Load:
## Fighting the Disappointment Bag

### *Let them know that failure and disappointment are coming.*

When my son was trying out for his middle school baseball team, I knew I had to ask him the question. On the night before the coach was posting the final cuts, I asked him, "What if you don't make the team?" It was a hard moment for me because I wanted him to know I believed in him. But I knew it was a real possibility, and I knew we needed to talk about how he would feel and what we would do if he didn't achieve this goal he had set for himself.

As parents, part of our job is to prepare our kids for both success and failure. When we can, we need to gently let them know that disappointment and failure are coming their way and they need to be prepared to deal with it. We don't want to scare them into worrying about it and push them to develop a negative attitude toward life and its opportunities, but we do need to help them be realistic. If they don't see potential disappointment coming, they may be thrown for a loop when it does.

### *Remind them that failure, disappointment, and perseverance are not only coming, but they are a part of the journey.*

Failure and disappointment are not to be feared. We don't want to pursue them, but they will invariably come. Unfortunately, many of us as parents struggle to receive the disappointment that comes with life. We may ignore the pain that comes with it or, worse, try

153

to numb it with all kinds of distractions. We've already shared this Scripture, but it's worth repeating. Paul reminds us the failure and disappointments that come our way are a part of our formation process. Romans 5:3-5 says, "Not only so, but we also glory in our sufferings, because we know that suffering produces perseverance; perseverance, character; and character, hope. And hope does not put us to shame, because God's love has been poured out into our hearts through the Holy Spirit, who has been given to us."

The disappointments and pain our kids feel should push them to persevere. This perseverance produces in them authentic character that leads to a hope that leads us again back to God. When they are in the middle of the disappointments of life, we have to remind them that it's all a part of God's process of growing and strengthening them. With his power and help, they can get through it. They can live to fight another day.

***Let them fail and deal with difficult situations. Don't bail them out!***

We have a friend who started down a dark path when he was in high school. He got involved with the "wrong crowd" and was soon buying, using, and selling some hard-core drugs. His parents agonized over their son's choices for years. They had raised him in the church and modeled a real relationship and life with Jesus. As he moved in and out of different rehab programs and facilities, there were times when his parents chose not to bail him out. They didn't break off ties or end their relationship, but they allowed him to experience the natural consequences of his decisions. As many recovery programs state, some people need to reach "rock bottom" and feel the weight of their choices before any real change can come. After years of trouble and pain, the young man began to make a turn and he is thriving in so many ways today.

This story is certainly extreme, but the principle applies. Our kids will never learn how to face and grow from disappointment if they don't ever have to go through it. Don't bail them out of situations in school, sports, with their friends, or at work. Help them navigate, but don't bail them out. There are way too many parents who are right in the middle of difficult situations with dating, sports, school, and friendships.

When they get a bad grade because they didn't do the work, don't reach out to the teacher. Make them do it. When they are running late for work or practice because they lost track of time, don't call or text their boss or coach to let them know. Make them do it. When they are struggling with a friendship or dating relationship, don't call the other party's parents to strategize or build a plan. Let them work it out. Coach them through it (as much as they'll let you) but let them work it out. We have to remember that disappointment and failure are not the enemies or the end of the world. It's simply a part of life that we all have to learn to deal with.

### When they fail, help them process why they failed.

Oftentimes when kids fail at something, they do not have the capacity or maturity to properly process why they failed. They may have an unrealistic view of their skills or abilities. They sometimes make mistakes they can't (or won't) see. They can view themselves as the victim who has been treated poorly, and their entitlement mentality can lead them to feel like they deserve something they haven't earned. For several reasons, our kids, teens, and young adults do not understand why they fail.

Helping them navigate these inevitable failures is critical to their long-term growth and health. To be positioned to help them, we first have to have a close relationship with them. We've talked about the importance of relationships. We then have to be willing to ask the right questions and lead them to see things they might not normally see.

We can ask questions like:

- Were the questions on the test really unfair? Do you really think you gave your best effort in studying?

- Does the coach really not like you, or are there other players who have been working harder and are maybe just better than you?

- Is that girl really mean, or have you possibly done or said some things that would cause her to treat you that way?

Again, we can only effectively ask questions like these in the context of a close relationship, and we have to work hard to have these conversations in love and not from a spirit of criticism or condemnation. Our kids have to believe we genuinely want to help them grow and learn how to process in a healthy way.

### *Model healthy ways to deal with disappointment.*

In one focus group, a young adult said, "I don't know how to process these things I'm going through because I never saw my dad struggle." As parents, we have to be careful how much we share our own struggles with our children. But we don't want to give them the false picture that everything in our life is perfect either. It can sometimes be appropriate to talk with our children about disappointments and struggles we have been through and what mechanisms we found useful in helping us move past them.

One girl shared with me, "Seeing unhealthy coping mechanisms in my family made me feel like I couldn't have emotions and express them, and I didn't learn how to cope." Not only do we not want to hide all of our struggles, but we also need to make sure we are modeling healthy ways to deal with the difficulties and disappointments we as parents face. It's okay for us to allow our emotions to spill out for our kids to see, as long as we don't dump these emotions on them and expect them to fix everything for us.

### *Create an atmosphere where your child feels safe sharing their feelings.*

I'm sure at this point you are tired of reading this but, again, relationships are key. Our kids need a place to express the pain of the disappointments they feel. One college student shared, "Often when I had issues I wanted to talk about, my parents didn't want to talk about it. I never learned how to express emotions." There is no doubt that, as our kids get older, the focus of parenting shifts. In the early years, the exhaustion is more physical due to sleep deprivation, along with chasing, bathing, clothing, feeding, and holding them. In the teen, college, and young adult years, the exhaustion becomes more mental and emotional. Conversations are difficult and the right ones don't happen when we want them to happen. We can't just schedule that talk about what our kids are disappointed about. When they are ready to talk, the opportunity presents itself whether we are ready or not.

Do everything you can to create an atmosphere where your kids feel comfortable talking to you about their failures and disappointments. There is no formula to this, and each child is different for sure. Model sharing your feelings, so your kids get used to this practice. Obviously, be careful and don't use your kids as your counselor or put them in a situation they cannot handle, but do set up a culture of sharing safely and productively.

### *Don't make them feel like* **they** *are a disappointment or failure.*

As I've already mentioned, this bag is closely tied to a lot of other bags, but when it comes to feeling like a disappointment, it's directly related to rejection. We need to do everything we can to never make our kids feel like we reject them, and we believe they are a disappointment or failure. Doing this will break the relationship in a big way and give them some baggage they may never unpack. Our words and actions matter. Like other parts of this section, navigating this can be tricky. Our kids sometimes need to feel the pain of disappointment because of a decision they have made. We just need to take extra caution not to push them over the line where they begin to tell themselves *they* are a disappointment.

### *Tell your kids you love them and are proud of them—a lot!*

One practical way to make sure your kids don't feel like they are a disappointment is to help them feel the opposite with both your words and your actions. Tell your kids you love them and you are proud of them and tell them these two things often. As they grow and journey through life, they are wondering how we feel about them. I never want my kids to doubt my love for them and I never want them to feel like I view them as a disappointment. I may be disappointed in them at times, and it's okay for them to feel that. We all just have to dance the dance of pushing them to see where they can improve while helping them develop a healthy sense of who they are. It's tricky!

When you are praising your kids, celebrate the small things. It's often easy to have a party when they graduate or accomplish a big goal. What about when they do the dishes or help their sibling with something? We should point out where they are growing and maturing in the everyday parts of life. If they consistently hear you building them up, they will be less likely to see themselves as a failure or disappointment.

## Wrapping up the Disappointment Bag

As I sat down to finish this chapter an interesting thought came to mind. After college, I moved back home to live with my parents. They had a large third-floor space that was all mine. I had a job as a youth director at a church, and I cruised along for several years. I don't think it was a "failure to launch" situation, but maybe it was. I remember having conversations with my dad at the kitchen table about when I was going to get a "real job" as he put it. Dad had been a successful businessman for years and had provided for our family in big ways. I, on the other hand, was perfectly content with my rather small salary and fun, exciting life as a youth pastor. I didn't have many bills and I was running fast and furious. I thought all was good.

But these conversations about making more money or being more productive would surface every so often. At that time of life, faith didn't seem important to dad, and he was certainly skeptical of the church. According to him, the church just wanted your money. As I navigated buying cars, thinking about buying a townhouse, and other worldly tasks, I often needed advice from dad, and he was glad to give it. That was in his wheelhouse. But looking back, I was looking not only for guidance from my dad but also affirmation. I do wonder if, for a while, I felt like a disappointment to him. He never outright said it, but I know I felt it.

I never did get a "real job." I stayed in full-time ministry, and I'm still there almost thirty years later. Now, if you are wondering, ministry is a "real job" in so many ways, but that's another conversation for another day. But I did see a shift in my dad's attitude about my profession of choice. Over the years, he began to value what I do. His change in attitude may have corresponded with his return to church, but something changed. I felt validated and like I had his approval. I've often said that we, as parents, need to pay attention to what is happening to our kids from age five to twenty-five to help them not pack these bags. I actually think the time frame may even be longer. I'm certain that my dad was not thinking about how to help me avoid the baggage of feeling like a disappointment, but that's what he did.

I share this story to let you know that it's never too late to fight this battle. Some parents who have heard this content feel bad about the thought that they've missed the boat in helping their kids lighten the load. I'm here to tell you—you haven't. You may be in a situation where you are simultaneously helping your kids (even if they are adults) unpack some bags while still trying to prevent them from packing at all. That seems to be what happened to me.

We need to remember the process I shared at the beginning of the book: encounter, formation, and expression. What we see, hear, and encounter in life helps to form who we become. How we are formed will always come out in what we do, what we say, and how we act. It will be the expression of our life. In some ways, this concept sits at the foundation of this book and definitely this chapter. We know our kids are going to encounter disappointment—it's just a matter of when and how much. Because of their inability to handle this failure and disappointment on their own (while their brains are still developing), we need to be there with them to help them with their formation. If we leave them to figure out how to deal with disappointment on their own, the expression might not be pretty. As we talked about this in one focus group, one young adult pointed out, "Not only do we feel like we are not enough and a disappointment, we rarely have anyone helping us get better."

Our job is to help them get better; not to shield them from disappointment and failure, but to help them get better at dealing with it. We have to be sufficiently close to our kids relationally but stay appropriately distanced from their problems and issues. We need to be involved (with their processing) while staying uninvolved (with their problems). Just typing all of that makes me dizzy. As with most things in parenting, it's messy. There is no clean and clear way to do this. It takes wisdom and discernment, and not just our own. We need to stay connected to God and ask Him to help us discern how to maneuver through these situations.

## Reflection Questions

What are some disappointments you have experienced in your life? What are some things you needed in those times to help you navigate the situation in a healthy way?

Have your kids ever seen you work through a struggle or disappointment? What did they see?

Have there been times when you swooped in to shield your child from dealing with disappointment. Do think this was helpful or hurtful? Is it hard for you to watch your kids experience disappointment? If so, why?

Why is it important to allow your kids to learn how to deal with disappointment? How can you help them understand the perspective that there is purpose in trials? Can you think of a time when your kids experienced disappointment? How did or can you help them process what is happening?

When was the last time you told your children you are proud of them? How can you make this encouragement become a regular part of your conversation with them? What is something small you can celebrate about your kids today?

# Endnotes

[1] https://www.weareteachers.com/lawnmower-parents/.

[2] Ibid.

[3] https://pittsburgh.citymomsblog.com/mom/rise-lawnmower-parent/.

[4] Sarah Young, *Jesus Calling,* Thomas Nelson, 2011, 25.

## Chapter Ten
# Lightening the Load

*"We're afraid to unpack our bags because we know what's in there."—college student*

As I progressed along in this project, I found myself seeking validation. I want to make sure that what I am presenting is valid, true, and real. I want to create something that can be helpful, not just to parents, but to a generation of kids and young adults. Maybe my quest for credibility comes from some sort of Performance or Comparison Bag I have packed in the past. I'm working on that.

One morning about halfway through writing this book I met with a college student. It was his 20th birthday and we had met off and on for a few years. His family was a part of our church, and I knew them all pretty well. His parents had been struggling through a separation and both this young man and his sister were having a hard time processing their thoughts. A statement he made during our conversation threw me for a loop. I was shocked, not totally because of the magnitude of the statement itself, but more because it was almost the exact statement I had heard from another young adult at the beginning of my research. He said, "I'm not sure that relationships can be successful. It's just too much work for too much heartbreak."

I had such a weird reaction to his statement. On the one hand, I was so sad for him and where I believe this thought process will lead him to in his future. We talked about that, a lot. On the other hand, I laughed a little. Crazy, I know. His statement bolstered me and gave me more confidence that this baggage stuff is for real, and we *have* to pay attention to it all.

In a lot of ways, this is a book about relationships—the relationships we *need* to have with our kids. As I mentioned in the first chapter of the book, one young adult told me, "We really need our parents to take the time to learn and understand the source of our baggage." If we have a growing relational distance between us and our kids, we'll have no shot at helping them see their baggage and fight against it. We have to work hard to be in a position to have the right conversations at the right times. One young adult told me, "Parents don't have the relational equity to have the right conversations. They have authority, but not the relational equity to talk about real things." When it comes to how our kids will turn out, the status of our relationship matters, and it matters a lot.

If we can build and maintain solid relationships with our kids, we'll have more of an opportunity to have the right conversations along the way. One of the real benefits of working on this book for me has been the conversations I've had with my kids about emotional baggage. Early in the project I was talking about and writing the section on school performance. In that chapter, I told the story of my daughter feeling like she has to always have all "As" in school. During the week I was writing that section, I was on a father-son campout with my son who is a few years older than my daughter. During one part of the night, we were to take some time to share our prayer requests with each other. I asked my son to pray for me and writing the book. Having heard my wife and me talking about the particular story I was writing, the thirteen-year-old said, "Hey dad. You might need to be careful in trying to help Kylie not pack that Performance Bag. In the process, you might be packing another bag." I was having a conversation about emotional baggage with my teenager, and he got the concept.

Over the past few years, I've had many opportunities to talk to my kids about the bags they might be packing. Thinking through these bags and potential issues has not only given my wife and me an awareness about how to prevent these bags, but it's given my kids some tools to use in their journey as well. Since they know we are paying attention to these bags and trying to help them avoid packing them, they too have an awareness about it all. I pray they, as teens, are aiming toward building a healthy foundation when it comes to their relationships, emotions, and spirituality. I know I never had conversations with my parents about issues like these. Talk to your kids about bags, especially as they get into their teen years. They can grasp the concept and it will help them be on the lookout.

As you come to the end of this book, I hope and pray you don't feel overwhelmed. When I first began to explain my idea for this book to my wife, she would look at me with a bit of a blank stare. I felt like God had put this idea in my heart and head and I was excited about trying to get it all down on paper. But Karin just couldn't seem to get excited about it. She would kind of nod her head and tell me it sounded interesting, but I could tell her heart wasn't into it. After talking to her about it several times, she finally had an "a-ha" moment. This is not a book that bashes parents! She thought I had been describing the idea that we as parents are directly responsible for the emotional baggage our kids accumulate. That is not the case at all! In her mind, she couldn't get excited about the book because she thought it was going to be about everything we as parents have done or are doing wrong when it comes to our kids and how we should and could change. Who wants to read about that?!

When I finally explained it in a slightly different way, she began to understand it wasn't so much about how we as parents have missed the mark, but instead about how the culture our kids are growing up in has a substantial impact on their formation—and can cause some serious baggage. She understood that, as parents, we are in a unique position to help them navigate through their life experiences in a healthy, God-centered way. As the primary spiritual leaders for our kids, we are responsible for paying attention to the bags they are packing and we have to remember that, as they grow up and navigate life, so many people and circumstances contribute to their baggage. Please don't minimize this. Don't think, "It's no big deal! They'll be okay." They might be able to put on a happy face and survive life (to an extent), but if we simply allow life to run its course and our kids to pack some heavy bags, I can assure you, they will not be okay. They will head toward the anxiety and depression that so pervades our culture and they will miss out on the life God intends for them to live.

So, while this book is certainly *not* intended to be a criticism against our parenting techniques, the truth is we are the most influential people in our kids' lives and we have been given the responsibility of helping them become independent, healthy, Christ-following adults who contribute to the kingdom of God. We want them to enter their adult years being healthy emotionally, relationally, and spiritually. We play a significant role in who our children become. With this weighty responsibility, I want to leave you with a couple of important truths to help encourage and exhort you along the road of parenting that I hope you will remember and employ long after your children leave your home.

# Lightening Your Load

### *Truth 1: God's Grace*

Never forget that God has an unlimited amount of grace to extend to you. I am sure as you have read this book, just as I did as I was writing it, you have been confronted with some parenting mistakes you have already made. You may have found yourself saying, "Oops—I've done that!" You may have realized that you have indeed played a role in packing some bags, just as I'm sure your parents did with you. We are imperfect people who live in an imperfect world, and therefore we are destined to be imperfect parents. We are going to make mistakes. Fortunately for us, we have a God who is not surprised by this. He was aware this was going to happen before He even created us, yet He created us anyway. All along His plan was for us to receive forgiveness for our shortcomings through faith in the death and resurrection of His Son. Romans 8:1 tells us, "Therefore, there is now no condemnation for those who are in Christ Jesus." We don't have to walk around with the weight and guilt of our sin on our shoulders. We will not always act in the best interests of our kids. We will fall short. But God knows this, and He has a plan for it. He even tells us His grace is enough for us and His power is made perfect in our weaknesses (2 Corinthians 12:9).

Not only does God forgive us for the ways we fall short, but He also redeems our shortcomings and uses them for good. Romans 8:28 says, "And we know that in all things God works for the good of those who love Him, who have been called according to his purpose." "All things" include our missteps, even the ones we take with our children. God is sovereign and all things are under His control. We can rest in the knowledge that God's grace covers our sins and He will complete the good work He begins in those who believe, including our children (Philippians 1:6).

### *Truth 2: The Battle*

Do you ever feel like your home is a battleground? Truthfully, mine has been. When the kids were little, we battled over getting them to bed. At times, we have battled hormones. Other times, we have battled disrespect and disobedience. We are definitely in the middle of battling over screen time and curfew. I imagine most of you can relate.

I don't want to come off as super-spiritual, but *there is* a spiritual battle going on in your home. This is the second truth I hope you will grab on to. It is not something that is talked about that often in most churches, but Scripture makes it clear that there is more going on in this life than meets the eye.

Ephesians 6:12 states, "For our struggle is not against flesh and blood, but against the rulers, against the authorities, against the powers of this dark world and against the spiritual forces of evil in the heavenly realms."

First Peter 5:8 says, "Be alert and of sober mind. Your enemy the devil prowls around like a roaring lion looking for someone to devour."

John 10:10 tells us, "The thief comes only to steal and kill and destroy."

And that is exactly what the devil wants to do—to steal, kill, and destroy our children's identity, confidence, joy, and relationships. He uses shame, comparison, disappointment, and rejection, among other things, to achieve this objective. He essentially uses all the bags our kids pack to keep them from experiencing the abundant life Jesus promises them. The good news is, God has equipped us for this battle. He knows the enemy's strategies and how best to combat them. The rest of John 10:10 says, "I have come that they may have life, and have it to the full."

Second Corinthians 10:4 states, "The weapons we fight with are not the weapons of the world. On the contrary, they have divine power to demolish strongholds."

Ephesians 6:10-18 goes into detail on how we can "take your stand against the devil's schemes." But the one weapon I want to focus on is revealed in verse 18: "And pray in the Spirit on all occasions with all kinds of prayers and requests. With this in mind, be alert and always keep on praying for all the Lord's people."

### Truth 3: The Power of Prayer

I once heard a phrase that rocked my world as a pastor. It says, "Ministry without prayer is the highest form of arrogance." Ouch. To think I can do any kind of ministry without first giving it to God and asking for His direction is the peak of arrogance.

I have adapted that phrase to say, "Parenting without prayer is the highest form of arrogance." To think we can raise these guys and girls without the power of God is taking a role we are not equipped to handle. These kids are God's kids before they are our kids, and He cares about them more than we do. We have to remember that and spend time in prayer asking Him to lead and guide us as we lead and guide them.

This is the third truth I want to leave with you. Prayer is powerful and effective (James 5:16). While in each chapter I have given you several suggestions on how you can fight to keep your child from packing a specific bag, prayer should always be included in your approach. In chapter two, I shared a story about an exercise I went through years ago where I identified what I wanted most out of life. This exercise was prompted by reading Philippians 4:6-7, which says, "Do not be anxious about anything, but in every situation, by prayer and petition, with thanksgiving, present your requests to God. And the peace of God, which transcends all understanding, will guard your hearts and your minds in Christ Jesus." In chapter two, I focused on the peace part of this passage. We all want peace. Here, I want to remind us how we can ultimately get that peace. We get it by "presenting our requests to God." We get it through coming to God in prayer. Notice, we're not talking about getting what we are asking for through our prayers, we are talking about receiving a peace that is far greater than anything we have ever known.

In recent years, my wife was turned on to a book by Jodie Berndt called *Praying the Scriptures for Your Children*. She has used this book and its' principles not only to pray for our kids but for all of her prayer life. She has found that praying Scripture over our kids has not only made her prayer life more meaningful, but also fills her with hope and confidence even when she doesn't see immediate results. We encourage you to take time to reflect on verses you find as you pay attention to how your kids are developing. Pray specific Scriptures over your kids and ask God to lead them away from packing bags you see emerging.

## Final Thoughts

As I was putting the final words down for this project, I reflected on where I started. As this bags idea was being birthed, I shared the first iteration of this content at a seminar at a church I was working with. At the end of the seminar, after talking about most of the bags, I told the parents a few things.

I know there is a lot here and you might feel like you have a lot to "do" as you help your kids. It can be overwhelming. As you evaluate where your kids are and what bags they might be packing, maybe pick just one thing to work on at a time. If you might struggle yourself with talking poorly about authority, pay attention to that tendency and try to stop. If you push your kids to perform in sports by putting pressure on them to be great, maybe pay attention to that pattern and try to stop. There is no way we can remember all of this and work on it all at once. Start with a few things and return to the book often to add something else.

As you work through this book and determine how you might better help your kids, I'd love to help. We all need guides sometimes, and I'd love to be one of those for you. You can go to www. equipandencourage.com to connect with me and find more tools and resources that can help you along your parenting journey.

If you want to boil down a lot of what I have shared, here's what you need to do:

- Be aware.
- Ask questions.
- Listen.
- Build the relationship.
- Ask more questions.
- Pray for discernment and wisdom.
- Do what you can do.
- Keep praying.

### *"Bucky and Beans"*

As Bucky and I traveled down the highway, we had a great conversation. He had been gracious enough to join me on a day-long trip where I needed his advice and expertise on a potential investment. While I would call him a real friend, he has been so much more than that to me over the years. He's about ten years my senior and we have been doing life and ministry together for almost two decades. He has mentored me in so many ways, and I so appreciate his friendship and presence in my life.

We talked about family, faith, finances, retirement, sports, and church. We also talked about our bags. He told me a story of when he was somewhere around ten years old. He was having a hard time in school and was struggling to focus and get the grades his mom expected. He remembered having a conversation with his mom where she pointed out a man on their street who was doing some construction and digging a ditch. She told Bucky to take a good look at him and she said, "You need to get it together or you're going to be like that guy. Do you want to eat steak, or do you want to eat beans?"

Bucky thought, "steak." He likes steak, plus he understood what his mom was saying. In her attempt to motivate him to work harder in school, what she did was pack some real baggage he was still unpacking some fifty years later in my car. He decided he (and his family) would always be able to eat steak. For most of his adult life, he worked incredibly hard to be successful and provide for his family, and he accomplished that goal. He built businesses, traveled, made loads of money, and has everything he needs in retirement.

But he would say he did that at the detriment of all the key relationships in his life. He's in his mid-50s struggling with the baggage and ramifications of being so focused on performance and providing financially for his family. He has a solid marriage, two great kids who are married, a few grandkids, and he loves to paint. But I think painting gives you an abundance of time to think, and Bucky has been thinking about and dealing with his baggage.

I never knew Bucky's mom, but I know she loved him. I know she worked hard to provide for their family. I also know that she put something in front of her son, a target if you will. She painted a picture for him and gave him a story to write. Her story for her son was, "Don't dig ditches for a living. Work hard so you can eat steak."

Eating steak is a great thing (at least for me), but I think we need to tell our kids a better story. I think we need to paint a better picture. I think we need to help them see they don't have to pack and struggle with so much baggage. We have the opportunity to help them lighten the load and live in a way of grace and freedom. Their lives will not be perfect and free of pain, but they can be fulfilling and abundant. If we pay attention and help our kids travel through life with minimal baggage, we will leave a different kind of legacy that could be passed down from generation to generation. Our kids (and their kids) will experience the kind of life they long for and they will experience a peace from God that transcends all understanding.

Isn't that what we all want?

## Reflection Questions

Take some time to reflect on God's grace for you as a parent and write down some thoughts concerning your relationship with Him. Use these verses to encourage you as a parent.

> "But he said to me, 'My grace is sufficient for you, for my power is made perfect in weakness.' Therefore I will boast all the more gladly about my weaknesses, so that Christ's power may rest on me" (2 Corinthians 12:9).

> "I pray that out of his glorious riches he may strengthen you with power through his Spirit in your inner being, so that Christ may dwell in your hearts through faith. And I pray that you, being rooted and established in love, may have power, together with all the Lord's holy people, to grasp how wide and long and high and deep is the love of Christ, and to know this love that surpasses knowledge— that you may be filled to the measure of all the fullness of God.

Now to him who is able to do immeasurably more than all we ask or imagine, according to his power that is at work within us, to him be glory in the church and in Christ Jesus throughout all generations, for ever and ever! Amen" (Ephesians 3:16-21).

"Therefore, there is now no condemnation for those who are in Christ Jesus, because through Christ Jesus the law of the Spirit who gives life has set you free from the law of sin and death" (Romans 8:1-2).

Take some time to reflect on what God has said to you as you have read this book. How can you be more intentional about praying for your kids as they grow up? Write down any final thoughts you may have.